VERB

Verbal Self Defense

in

The Workplace

Dr. Daniel Scott, Msc.D.

bookshaker

bookshaker

First Published in Great Britain 2010
www.bookshaker.com

I dedicate this book to Izumi Hiroaki Sensei… who taught me more than the fundamental principles of Aikido - he taught me to live my dreams.

ACKNOWLEDGEMENTS

I would like to give my deepest heartfelt thanks to:

Judy Wright for unlocking the secrets of NLP, sharing her boundless wisdom & experience, mentoring me through endless growing pains, and ultimately awakening me to a greater purpose in life.

Christo Georgiev for his inspiration and encouragement to develop my original idea for a 6 step model of verbal self defense.

The entire NLPU 2004 Trainer and Consultancy Certification class for all the feedback and guidance they gave me in order to create an NLP-based form of verbal self defense.

Nelson Johnston and Gwen Pasveer who provided me with a place and opportunity to practice these new techniques of verbal self defense.

Julie Salisbury, creator of the "InspireABook" book building system (www.InspireABook.com), who gave me the personal coaching and connections that I needed in order to make this book a reality.

My family and friends, especially Vaughn, Jodie and Brenda for their never-ending patience and unwavering belief in both me and my dream - without which I never would have gotten through all the hardships and setbacks we had along the way.

DISCLAIMER

This book is designed to provide information on verbal self defense tactics. It is sold with the understanding that the publisher and author are not engaged in rendering legal or professional counseling services. If legal or other expert assistance is required, the services of a competent professional should be sought. This information is based on the author's own research carried out to develop tactics for verbally defending himself. It is not the purpose of this book to reprint all the information that is otherwise available to the general public, but instead to complement, simplify and pass on the author's own first-hand experience. You are encouraged to read all other available material about verbal self defense for your own mental, emotional and physical safety and well-being.

Every effort has been made to make this book as complete and accurate as possible. However, there may be mistakes and therefore this text should be used only as a general guide, and not as the only guide to verbally defend yourself. The purpose of this book is to inspire you to take action towards developing your own skills and abilities for maintaining your personal health and wellness in situations where contact with verbally abusive people are present. Or to seek out further information in regards to gaining assistance from other sources in your community to help you ensure your personal safety and well-being from potentially harmful verbal aggressors in your life.

Any and all tips, tool, techniques and advice provided in this book are intended to offer simple awareness of communication tactics used successfully by the author. Many factors will be important in determining your actual results and no guarantees are made that you will achieve results similar to anyone else's, and in fact no guarantees are made that you will achieve any results from the ideas and concepts covered within this book.

The Author shall have neither liability nor responsibility to any person or entity with respect to loss or damage caused, or alleged to have been caused, directly or indirectly, by the information contained in this book.

If you do not wish to be bound by the above, you may return this book to the person or company you bought it from for a full refund.

Praise for Verbal Self Defense

"I really appreciate your book - I am getting a little frustrated with the victim-mentality out there and the idea that targets don't play an active role in their own circumstances. So, thank you for offering up some real and tangible advice about communication - which provides empowerment, as opposed to counseling - which facilitates the victim-mentality."

Catherine Mattice, MA
Workplace Bullying Expert
www.noworkplacebullies.com

"Dr. Scott's book is a must-read for anyone who feels they are being verbally bullied at work. The book offers practical advice, guidelines and exercises for evaluating and dealing effectively with workplace bullies. You'll learn how to stop feeling powerless and start using effective verbal defense strategies to resolve conflict."

Janet Attard,
www.businessknowhow.com

"Daniel's use of explaining his '6 steps' simply allows for the reader to gain ready insight into effective tools he or she can apply to everyday occurrences in and out of the office."

Drew Van Brunt, MSW
Separation & Divorce Coach
Victoria, BC

"There's a point where 'I'm sorry' becomes insulting."

R.K. Milholland
Something Positive (S*P)

CONTENTS

OVERVIEW **1**

PART I: YES, IT WILL WORK FOR YOU **7**

FEELING GOOD ABOUT FEELING BAD 17

A SENSE OF SAFETY IN KNOWING 22

THE BRAIN OF YOUR EXISTENCE 28

PART II: GET OUT OF MY SHOES **43**

WELL I THINK… 47

I KNOW, YOU THINK … 57

ALL THE ON-LOOKERS THINK… 72

PART III: KNOW YOUR SELF **85**

ARE YOU UPSET ABOUT SOMETHING? 88

WHAT ARE YOU TRYING TO SAY? 102

SO, WHAT DO YOU WANT FROM ME? 118

PART IV: CONTROL YOUR SELF **133**

KEEPING BALANCE IN MIND 136

STATE… WHAT YOU WANT 144

MAKING THE RIGHT CONNECTIONS 153

PART V: USING VERBAL SELF DEFENSE 159

A FLUID 3 POINT BASE 162

THE 6 STEPS OF VERBAL SELF DEFENSE 167

STEPPING UP IN THE REAL WORLD 180

PUTTING IT ALL TOGETHER 191

PART VI: BEYOND VERBAL SELF DEFENSE 203

A LITTLE MORE OR LESS... 206

...IT'S ALL THE SAME 217

APPENDICES 223

A: MANAGERS AND SUPERVISORS 224

B: CUSTOMERS AND CLIENTS 228

C: CO-WORKERS AND TEAM MEMBERS 232

D: EMPLOYEES, STAFF AND PERSONNEL 236

FOREWORD

The other day I had a conversation with a martial arts instructor and dear friend. As we discussed my interest in workplace bullying and his interest in martial arts, he talked about training his students to act, rather than react.

When you act, he explained, you are aware of your instincts and the importance of overcoming them. To act means to recognize the situation you are in, understand what it means for you, become aware of your feelings, apply your consciousness, and choose your actions carefully. Conversely, react is an instinctual, indulgent, gut-feeling, auto-motor defense that usually results in making the wrong decision. Act means to block and prepare to fight; react means to punch without making plans for the aftermath.

A few days later I met Dr. Scott. Needless to say I was delighted to see that someone else was thinking what I was thinking - responding to bullies needs to be an action, not a reaction. Action would mean careful consideration of how to respond to when you find yourself in the evil clutches of a bully. It would mean to block and prepare to communicate with confidence and competence. Reaction would mean letting the anger and hurt take over. Unfortunately, the later doesn't offer many options other than defeat.

For the last 25 years or so, academics in the fields of organizational behavior and psychology, social psychology, business management, occupational health, and workplace safety have been researching the concept of workplace bullying. Consistently, they find between 50-70% of people in the workforce around the world have been bullied at some point during their working lives. They also continue to find that these negative behaviors are extremely damaging to the targeted individuals, the co-workers who witness them, and the organization as a whole.

All scholars agree that bullying is caused by a variety of things working together that ultimately include organizational factors, and target and bully personality and predisposition. Relatively few scholars, however, have addressed the role targets play in the process of bullying and most even advise against taking such perspectives. The general consensus seems to be that targets are "accidental victims" in an "accidental situation", that victims are irrelevant and work conditions are the primary source of the bullying, and that the bully and the organization are at fault thereby eradicating the target of any role in the process of bullying at work.

Certainly blaming targets is unprincipled, but ignoring the active role they play in a relationship with a co-worker is erroneous and precludes them from taking empowering action against their abusers. Bullying must be explored as an ongoing relationship and communication transaction, rather than a one-sided exchange where victims are simply innocent passers-by in their own life at work - that leaves them no empowering options at all and perpetuates victimization. While bullying is certainly not the target's "fault" it is important to understand that in every relationship each person plays a very active part, whether with a romantic partner, family member, extraordinarily nice co-worker, or workplace bully.

This book is an important contribution to the field of workplace bullying because it provides tools for self-discovery that go beyond assertiveness training, self-esteem or self-help. Dr. Scott gives readers the knowhow to take control of their minds, emotions and reactions, and thus their situations. You cannot control the bully, but you can control your intrapersonal and interpersonal communication. You can take control of the circumstances with your actions.

To my knowledge, Dr. Scott is the only person looking at workplace bullying through the extremely powerful lens of Neuro Linguistic Programming (NLP). He has done a wonderful job of translating the concepts and teachings of NLP into tangible and easy-to-read information that anyone can use for a successful fight against their workplace bully. The book also provides several valuable exercises and a whole lot of concrete advice that can be applied immediately.

This is a wonderful and practical guide for dealing with the workplace bully. As managers and human resources continue to ignore the problem of bullying, it becomes particularly important that we arm targets with the resources needed to successfully maneuver through work. "Here, here!" to advocates of victim accountability and the resulting empowerment. People like Dr. Scott facilitate a target's own quest for positive change at work and in life through consciousness, communication, and other such tools. Counseling, a current popular method for targets seeking to change their situation, leaves "victims" exactly that - helpless passerby's in their own lives.

Catherine M. Mattice, MA
Consultant: Subject Matter Expert in Workplace Bullying
www.NoWorkplaceBullies.com

AN OVERVIEW OF VERBAL SELF DEFENSE

The basic fact is that anyone can be a bully, and anyone can be bullied. No matter who you are, there are people that are smaller and meeker than you. In the same sense, no matter how big or mean a bully is, there will always be someone somewhere in this world who is bigger, meaner, quicker and tougher than they are. So, the thing that will truly define a workplace bully is not their ability to intimidate or push people around, it's their ability to choose their victims wisely.

Usually the best type of person to pick on is milder in some way that the bully can use to their advantage. As an example, people who are emotionally victimized will often be socially inexperienced and subsequently not know how to handle public teasing, etc. Alternatively, a victim who constantly suffers mental attacks probably can't think quickly enough to defend themselves against an onslaught of a bully's pre-prepared insults. An expert bully will even go so far as to ensure their victims are physically smaller than them. The reason for this is so they can use aggressive posturing to intimidate the person into submission if the emotional teasing or mental taunting fails to achieve their desired results.

WHERE VERBAL SELF DEFENSE CAME FROM

These were the characteristics which made me the perfect 'bully-magnet' growing up. Since I suffered from acute asthma I was sick all the time, so I missed a lot of school and social functions. As a result it made me a small, foolish, social outcast - the term 'victim' personified.

That was before I discovered Aikido. First and foremost this is a martial art built around breathing techniques (which are great for asthmatics who want to strengthen their respiratory systems). As well, Aikido teaches you how to physically deal with attackers in order to defend yourself. Truthfully, I never needed to use my fighting skills, just knowing them increased my sense of self-confidence.

It was then that I met my first sensei, Dr. Hiroaki Izumi, who was more than just a magnificent Aikido instructor; he was also my first mentor. He taught me many lessons that transcended martial arts and had a deep impact on all aspects of my life. Through the principles of Aikido, Izumi Sensei showed me how to physically and mentally handle any adversity life could present. It was during his many teachings that he once told me to, "Do what you love and allow the money to come".

Through following that advice I eventually met Judy Wright who first introduced me to the behavioral science of Neuro Linguistic Programming (NLP). With her instruction I was able to develop my understanding of human behavior and exponentially increase my abilities to effectively communicate with others and influence the course of my life. Having received my NLP Practitioner and Master Practitioner Certification from Judy I finally felt ready and able to take full control over my life.

Continuing on my chosen path I attended NLP University in 2004 - the place where everything would come together and give birth to the concept of a 6-step model for verbal self defense. In the NLP Trainer and Consultancy Certification program I had the opportunity to work with and receive input from NLP trainers from around the world. Utilizing their ongoing feedback I began to create innovative, new techniques for verbal self defense using combinations of NLP language patterns and principles of Aikido. With constant encouragement from so many wise and wonderful people I finally put together the very first 6-step verbal self defense model. The end result was a process which could help people appropriately and professionally handle both verbal and non-verbal abuse at work and at home.

Upon my return to Canada I was given the opportunity to take a security position at the Cambie Bar & Grill at the Esquimalt Inn in Victoria, BC. This was where the 6-step verbal self defense model was first field-tested over the course of 2 years. During that time I was able to use my own first-hand experience to make the necessary adjustments which would ensure 'real life' effectiveness of the verbal self defense tactics and training you are going to learn in this book.

Why You're Here

I think it's safe to say we all agree that 'everyone' has times in life which are more difficult than others (which I realize may seem kinda obvious). Economic prosperity will continue to come and go. Children will be born and loved ones will die. People will get married and some will get divorced. Good times will be followed by bad times which will be followed by good times again. It's just one more cycle of life.

> ***High levels of stress can increase the chance of a person becoming verbally abusive without even realizing it.***

Everybody will find themselves in the midst of difficult times at some point in their life - situations which they seem to have little or no control over. That feeling of powerlessness can cause people to seek a sense of control wherever they can possibly find it. One simple example of this is someone experiencing financial difficulty, such as losing their job and having no way to pay their bills.

IMAGINE...

If someone has little or no money they will often face an endless barrage of tough decisions every day. Do you buy food or pay the rent? Take a second job to pay for daycare or try to cut expenses so one job will cover the bills?

These kinds of difficult choices will create high amounts of stress and can potentially lead to the person becoming so overwhelmed and upset that they will verbally lash out at anyone. In essence, these are good people in a bad situation who simply succumb to the pressures of life.

Any one of the many professionals they deal with every day could be the target of that anger and frustration. This includes everyone from the bill collectors who are constantly phoning, right down to the local convenience store clerk who can't sell them liquor because they left their identification at home.

In this example let's imagine that the electric company receives a phone call from a highly stressed person wanting to discuss having their power turned off. It's very possible that during this phone call the customer could turn abusive simply because the staff member does not have the authority to fix their problem.

Frustration, anger, annoyance, fear, uncertainty, along with a dozen other emotions can be too much to handle for them. The stress can turn a normally kind and calm person into a verbal bully. They may yell, scream, threaten, swear, and attempt to intimidate the employee in an effort to get their power turned back on. Although it's unlikely these tactics will get them the outcome they want, the fact remains that the person simply does not know any other way to deal with the situation and all the negative emotions they're feeling.

At the opposite end of the spectrum it's possible that certain people are simply just bullies. It's true - some people in this world just seem to be mean spirited. The fact is, even though they may not think of themselves as bullies, the things they say and do cause others mental and emotional pain and suffering.

In either case, whether it's intentional or not, you need a way to verbally defend yourself from anyone who is abusive. You need a set of tactics which you can easily remember and effortlessly apply in any instance of workplace bullying, and that's where the 6-step model for verbal self defense comes in.

What to Expect Now

I want to start by warning you that the basic components of effective verbal self defense we are going to explore in this book will involve a great deal of self-discovery and personal clarification. The most important are: identifying what bullying behavior is for *you;* how to spot it; and ways to stop it before it causes you to feel bullied.

In the process of returning to a position of power and control in situations of conflict you'll learn how to focus your mind and attention in order to strengthen your communication skills and abilities. Then you will take it even further in order to understand and avoid the mistake of mixing different points of view.

By freeing yourself from the limitations put on you by other people's perceptions you will develop greater self-control. In fact, you'll even go through a process to identify, clarify and build your own powerful mental and emotional 'state of mind' specifically designed for dealing with office bullies.

Your actual verbal self defense skills will start with a simple but effective 3 point base which will allow you to maximize the speed and flexibility of your thoughts. At the same time your base will help you maintain a solid sense of confidence in your ability to handle the situation. From the resulting well-formed foundation you can then easily and effortlessly follow the 6 steps for addressing any bullying type behaviors of others.

Going beyond the basic 6-step strategy for verbal self defense you will also learn advanced principles: for dealing with multiple attackers; handling conflict in different kinds of relationships (customers, supervisors, co-workers and subordinates); and even how to apply verbal self defense in different forms of communication, such as writing. As well, you'll learn supplementary techniques of verbal self defense which can be used together, in conjunction with the 6-step model, or as stand-alone tools and tactics all on their own.

The best part of all this is that at each step along the way you'll be given exercises so that you can practice the different skills and abilities you learn in each section of the book. So, now that you have the general idea of where we're going, let us begin your training…

PART I

YES, IT WILL WORK FOR YOU

"*Workplace bullying* is _____________." What? What *is* workplace bullying? Currently there is no single, clear definition and that means it can be kind of difficult to know how and when it happens.

We can all recognize bullies on a school playground - they work alone or in groups and they push, kick, point and laugh, pull people's pants down, ridicule and demean others, give wedgies, steal lunches, put frogs down girls' tops, etc. Hmmm… unless you work in some kind of lab the chances of co-workers having access to frogs seems quite minimal. So how do we spot 'workplace' bullies?

After we leave school, everyone usually adheres to a set of grown-up rules and, by extension, workplace rules; however, even within these rules workplace bullies still seem to find a variety of ways to bully people. And since bullying behavior can come in so many forms it seems almost impossible for researchers to agree on how to categorize 'harmful' versus 'non-harmful' interactions… which we can loosely translate into *okay-behaviors* compared to *not-okay-behaviors.*

Websites and books on the topic seem to agree that there is a fine line between 'strong management styles' and actual 'workplace bullying'. Yet, experts still cannot tell us how we are supposed to know when we are being bullied and (more importantly) when to take action to defend ourselves!

One thing agreed upon is the *Reasonable Person Test*. What this means is that when you are unsure if you are being bullied, ask yourself, "Would most people consider *what the other person is saying or doing* to be 'inappropriate' or 'unacceptable'?" If the reasonable person test determines that it's inappropriate or unacceptable then it can be treated like bullying and you can happily use your verbal self defense tactics.

For further clarification…

Recognizing Bullying Behavior

Although verbal (and non-verbal) abuse is a form of aggression, the actions can come in both obvious and subtle formats. Furthermore, it's important to remember that these are usually patterns of behavior rather than single isolated incidents.

Some examples of common workplace bullying:

- Spreading malicious rumors, gossip or innuendos.
- Excluding or isolating someone socially.
- Intimidation using words, tone of voice, gestures or body posture.
- Deliberately impeding a person's movements or ability to work.
- Threats of harm, including possible termination of employment.
- Unwarranted (or undeserved) punishment.
- Intruding on a person's privacy by pestering, spying or stalking.
- Doing things to cause someone feelings of guilt, shame or embarrassment.
- Yelling or using profanity.
- Persistently or constantly criticizing a person.
- Belittling a person's opinions.
- Assigning unreasonable expectations, duties or workload.
- Assigning too few duties or too little work, creating feelings of uselessness.
- Blocking applications for training, time off or promotions.
- Tampering with someone's personal belongings.
- Purposefully withholding necessary information or giving the wrong information.

To simplify, any behavior which leaves a person feeling bad about themselves, about their relationship with someone else, or about the organization in general is technically abusive in nature. Although feelings of abuse are not usually the intention of the attacker it still remains an issue for the person who is left feeling bad.

This does NOT imply that anytime someone does something you feel is unacceptable it can be labeled as *bullying*. Instead, it is better to focus on dividing behaviors into two categories:

- Those that work toward building a positive working environment; and,
- Those more likely to create a general sense of discomfort and/or anxiety.

This is where we want to recognize that the result of bullying (negative feelings) and how bullies communicate (inappropriate words/actions) are different. If you think of verbal self defense as one particular 'style of communication' then when you're dealing with abusive or bullying behaviors the attacker would be using a different style, or a combination of different styles of communication.

When you're dealing with abusive or bullying behaviors, your attacker may use a particular style, or a combination of different styles of communication.

With the multitude of different ways people can choose to communicate (each having its own pros and cons) the most important comparison to make is how each style differs in its 'intention'. As you read the description for each of the following communication styles think about a time when you were spoken to in that manner, and remember how it made you feel at the time.

Persuasive Communication

A person may communicate with an intention to try and 'influence' you. When people are using persuasion tactics they are attempting to guide your thoughts toward the acceptance of an idea, attitude or action using forms of rationalization. What they are really trying to do is access something in your memory that will motivate you to make the decision they want you to make. Their goal is to connect what they want to something you desire so that it seems like a good idea to you.

An example is, "If you do this, you'll be more popular and you want to be popular, right?" However, the problem is that persuasive communication is not always logical because its goal is to strategically solve a problem by relying on appeals rather than facts or validity.

Argumentative Communication

An argument starts when one or more people begin to take the outcome of the discussion personally. When the topic of conversation challenges a person's deep sense of values, beliefs about the world, morality and/or personal identity, they will change their communication style to be more aggressive. The gist of an argument can usually be summed up as, "I'm right, you're wrong, and I'm going to prove it no matter what it takes!" Whenever both sides of the discussion take on this inflexible attitude the argument can break down and end without a solution.

It's interesting to note that commonly one person will usually give in when they deem the outcome of the argument more important than the meaning of that outcome. An example is when someone chooses to accept the label of being 'wrong' in order to avoid conflict in the relationship - that means the person puts more value on avoiding conflict over being identified as wrong.

Manipulative Communication

The intention behind a manipulative person is to get what they want no matter how it affects other people. A manipulator will do and say whatever they deem necessary to achieve their outcome. This allows their behaviors to become flexible to the point of lying and cheating. However, a manipulator may not consider what they do to be deceitful or wrong, but rather they may believe that the end justifies the means.

If a person values the outcome of an interaction more than their personal morals, then manipulative communication becomes an acceptable option. Thus, beyond seeing this style of communication in people who are selfish and self-centered, you also see manipulative tactics in situations of extreme misfortune such as a mother or father lying and cheating in order to feed their starving child.

Hostile Communication

Hostile communication is intended to teach someone a lesson. Often, people become hostile when they feel that they've been wronged in some way. A hostile aggressor justifies their behavior in their own mind by feeling they have been personally attacked, or by feeling a need to assert a sense of power or control where they feel there is none (especially if they feel it's been taken away from them). This includes someone saying or doing something that directly violates the person's sense of right and wrong - when somebody breaks their rules it's equivalent to sending the message, "I'm above your rules". The result will often be a need to 'teach the person a lesson'!

It's because of this, "I'm justified in doing this," perception that an aggressive or hostile communicator will usually remain unaware of the negative effects their words and actions have on the one they are communicating with. This is the main reason why people who are mentally and emotionally abusive have a difficult time changing.

Since what they say or do seems like the right idea at the time, then it will only be in hindsight that they realize how their behavior is 'bad' and consequently feel remorse for it. The concern is that the next time a similar situation comes up they will likely do the same thing again because in that moment it will still seem like their only option. In order to change their hostile communication tactics the person must be aware of better choices before the same situation happens again.

Defensive Communication

A person using a defensive style of communication takes time to recognize the effect hostile communication has on them, and then they focus only on addressing the attack and NOT the attacker. Defensive communication really only exists when there is a sense of being attacked, because without a sense of being attacked defensive communication will only amount to a form of persuasion. For this reason verbal self defense is a lot like physical self defense because you only take physical action to defend yourself when there is an actual physical attack. Thus, verbal self defense is something you will only use when you feel mentally or emotionally attacked by a person's words, tone of voice, physical posturing, gestures, facial expressions, insinuations, etc.

IMAGINE...

Picture in your mind a person walking down the street and, as they pass a doorway, a gentleman taps them on the shoulder and asks, "May I borrow a quarter for the phone?" Would you feel it's appropriate for the person to respond by immediately turning and punching the gentleman in the face?

Alternatively, imagine the same person walking down the street on a bright, sunny day and, as they pass a doorway, a gentleman grabs the person forcefully by the arm, pushes them up against the wall, and smacks them in the face yelling, "Give me a quarter for the phone before I kick your head in dummy!" In this case one might consider physical defense a reasonably appropriate response against being pushed around and slapped.

To put this in perspective, let's compare these examples to someone asking for the time. If a stranger said, "Excuse me, do you know what time it is?" we can assume verbal self defense is a bit of an extreme response. However, if the stranger said, "Hey stupid, what time is it?" then verbal self defense could be an acceptable means of handling the situation, specifically dealing with the insult of being called stupid.

In the examples above, the key is whether or not the defender has a sense of being attacked. If you do not feel threatened or hurt by the person's behavior (in this example, if you don't take being called 'stupid' as a personal insult) then there is no need to defend yourself, is there?

In order to be absolutely certain that verbal self defense is going to work for you, just like physical self-defense, it requires you to learn and practice a new set of skills. This all begins by developing a way of recognizing what mental and emotional attacks are to you.

Rather than simply labeling generalized situations, behaviors or words as being 'abusive', 'inappropriate' or 'offensive' it's better to learn how your own mind and body tells you when something is unacceptable. Once you understand how and why an attacker's words and/or actions are abusive to you it then becomes possible to develop your own plan to defend yourself.

You wouldn't dream of stepping into a boxing match without preparing, and for the same reason it's very important to practice your verbal self defense.

Being able to identify what bullying is in your own mind is extremely important because your personal values change depending on the context of the situation or the people involved. For example, you might be a lot more forgiving of certain behaviors from someone who has been your best friend since elementary school compared to somebody that you met last week. In the workplace it may be more likely you will accept certain things from a long-time boss or supervisor compared to what you would accept from a new assistant.

No matter what kind of attack you're presented with or who it comes from, verbal self defense is going to give you guidelines for effectively dealing with it. All the tools and techniques in this book will be explained and then you will learn how you can practice them in safety (away from situations of conflict, before an attack occurs). The goal is to practice them in such a way that they will become a part of your natural habits of self defense.

The key to achieving that is, just like you would not dream of stepping into a boxing match without preparing, it is just as important to practice all the skills you learn in this book. As with anything new, it may feel awkward, difficult and perhaps even a little silly at first, but stick with it and your verbal self defense skills and abilities will soon become a part of how you naturally communicate.

You might be asking, "How do you know that for sure?" The answer is quite simple - all the tools, techniques and exercises in this book have been designed using the behavioral science of Neuro Linguistic Programming (NLP). Everything has been created in a way that will allow your brain to learn these skills as easily and effortlessly as possible. So much so, that, when you are well-versed in verbal self defense, your unconscious behaviors will actually help to teach your attacker how to be a better communicator. (Didn't know you could do that, did you?)

In the meantime - there is no escaping the truth - workplace bullies create unhealthy working environments. We all know that, whatever form it comes in, workplace bullying always leaves people feeling bad, but the questions to ask are: "Why does it make us feel bad?" and, "What do we learn about ourselves when we are bullied?"

Learning to answer those questions will become the source of your power in verbally defending yourself. Using that knowledge you can build your own personalized verbal defense tactics which you know work best for you. How you develop that knowledge and use it as a power source begins with discovering what your own, personal reactions mean, and how to parlay that wisdom into the best possible response(s) to bullying in your workplace.

With that in mind, let's get started ...

DEVELOPING YOUR SKILLS & ABILITIES…

IDENTIFYING YOUR NEGATIVE EMOTION LABELS

The following is a list of negative emotions that people use to describe what they are feeling. Begin by remembering an incident at work that left you feeling bad, wishing you could go back and change.

As you recall that event, go through the list below and check off all the things that you felt during the actual event. There are a few blank spaces at the end to add any other descriptive feelings you want to use.

□ Fearful	□ Tense	□ Anxious
□ Afraid	□ Nervous	□ Worried
□ Concerned	□ Scared	□ Insecure
□ Shame	□ Demeaned	□ Rejected
□ Worthless	□ Useless	□ Inadequate
□ Insignificant	□ Unimportant	□ Ignored
□ Left out	□ Humiliated	□ Despicable
□ Pathetic	□ Hurt	□ Dejected
□ Depressed	□ Melancholy	□ Sorrowful
□ Dismal	□ Despondent	□ Down
□ Gloomy	□ Glum	□ Forlorn
□ Low	□ Angry	□ Frustrated
□ Annoyed	□ Irritated	□ Perturbed
□ Ticked off	□ Livid	□ Outraged
□ Furious	□ Seething	□ Venomous
□ Aggravated	□ Perturbed	□ Insulted
□ Resentful	□ Indignant	□ Guilty
□ Judged	□ Undeserving	□ Disgraceful
□ Remorseful	□ Lonely	□ Abandoned
□ Hollow	□ Empty	□ Bleak
□ Alone	□ Withdrawn	□ Detached
□ Distant	□ Desolate	□ Despair
□ Hopeless	□ Agony	□ Anguish
□ Helpless	□ Defeated	□ Destitute
□ Deficient	□ Unlucky	□ Mad
□ Resentful	□ Enraged	□ Anxious
□ Worried	□ Nervous	□ Discouraged
□ Uneasy	□ Foolish	□ Concerned
□ Flustered	□ Overwhelmed	□ Desperate
□ Tense	□ Pressured	□ Self-conscious
□ ______________	□ ______________	□ ______________
□ ______________	□ ______________	□ ______________

Now think about how often these feelings happen at work. Is it rare, occasional or perhaps, often? What might it be like to be able to create a working environment where you know that you will never feel those negative feelings? Think about how great that will be and imagine how much you will love what that experience is going to be like.

FUNDAMENTAL LESSONS & LEARNINGS...

- The most important thing to notice about different styles of communication is their intention.
- Just like physical self defense, verbal self defense requires you to practice the skills you learn.
- Practicing the exercises in this book, which are based on techniques of NLP, will help install the skills of verbal self defense as an unconscious habit.

FEELING GOOD ABOUT FEELING BAD

"Everything that irritates us about others can lead us to an understanding of ourselves."
Carl Jung

CONGRATULATIONS! YOU'VE BEEN BULLIED!

Having someone congratulate you for getting bullied seems like an odd way to consider it, doesn't it?

Stereotypically psychologists are supposed to say, "The first step to getting better is admitting you have a problem." However, the immediate retort in our situation might be, "No! It's their problem because they are the ones doing the bullying!"

You're right... and it affects you, does it not? It leaves you feeling hurt, angry, sad, or maybe even a bit like wanting to shove a stapler up their nose, right? So, the good news is (hence the 'congratulations') that the bullying, or rather, your reaction to it, is teaching you something amazing about yourself.

This is the opportunity to learn about what you really need in order to be happy in life. The bad news is that, unless you listen to your inner reactions and do something about them, those negative feelings will eventually start working against you.

To begin, it's necessary to recognize that the feelings you experience when you are being bullied, hurt or insulted should not be a normal part of your everyday life. Sadly, they're common, but should certainly not be normal everyday living conditions. Not only are you entitled to be happy in life, but you are entitled to be happy at work too (I know… kinda seems hard to imagine sometimes). After all, having a joyful life is truly the ultimate goal - yes, really, it's true - I read it in a book somewhere.

So how do we create this joyful existence when there is bullying in our lives? Before we can actually do anything about the bullying we need to understand why we feel the way we do after being bullied. We are human and, as such, we are driven to do things that feel good. This desire to feel good can be divided into two types of motivation:

> 1) We already feel pretty good, but want it to be even better. For example, we are in a fantastic mood so we spend time doing our favorite hobby, or we buy something special for ourselves, or turn up our favorite song in the car and sing along like no one is watching.
>
> 2) We feel lousy, ill-done by, like something's missing, miserable so we look for things to do which will get our good feelings back up to where we think they should be. For example, a depressed person might eat, sleep, drink, exercise, buy things, clean, break stuff or maybe yell at and belittle others.

The point to remember here is that all negative feelings and emotions exist for a reason. Feelings such as fear tell us when we're in danger. Anger is a sign that we need to protect something. Sadness and hurt offer us an awareness of what is important to us. The purpose of every negative emotion is to help us to recognize our own beliefs and values in life and to do what's necessary to keep them safe.

Some psychologists call these beliefs and values one's *Personal Boundaries*. When someone's words or actions are in direct conflict with what you define as appropriate or what is 'right' this is called a *Boundary Violation,* and it will generate a negative feeling inside you. In this way you can think of negative emotions like giant internal spotlights created in your unconscious mind - they're trying to get your conscious mind to focus its attention on a specific problem.

If we could translate negative emotions into words, your unconscious mind might say something like, "Hey! Look over here! Yes - that's right - follow those feelings of anger over here. See what's happening here? This is one of our deeply-held personal beliefs, and what's going on here is NOT ok with us. So, do something that will fix it immediately - I want to feel good again, right now!"

> ***The intention of a negative emotion is to spur us to do something to make the bad feeling go away.***

This loss of good feelings (mental, emotional or physical) can range from slight discomfort or annoyance to major trauma or heartbreak. How important the violated belief or value is to you will determine the level and intensity of the negative emotion(s) you feel.

Beneath the surface, the unconscious goal or purpose of a negative emotion is commonly defined in NLP jargon as its *Highest Positive Intent.* The concern is that the intention of a negative emotion will spur us to do something to make the bad feeling go away even if that *something* leads to problems later on. The mind only focuses on finding a way to feel better *now*! Whatever the outward reaction is that we have in the moment, our unconscious mind considers it to be the best and most efficient way to alleviate the cause of the negative emotion and put our feelings back in balance.

IMAGINE...

Two office clerks are talking about a missing client file when the senior clerk makes the comment, "Obviously you're not putting the files back where they belong."

Feeling personally attacked, the junior clerk reacts abruptly by replying in an angry tone of voice, "Well you aren't perfect either, you know!"

The ensuing argument which escalates into snide remarks and rude comments will later be considered as both unprofessional and inappropriate - especially in their boss's opinion.

Let's delve into the Junior Clerk's reaction in the example above as if we can actually read his mind. Junior believed that Senior's choice of words was insinuating that Junior is unable or unwilling to do his job properly. As a result, Junior felt he needed to defend his personal identity as a good employee (and consequently, a good person).

Being able to read his mind allows us to know that Junior puts a lot of value on good work ethics. However, we can also tell that being perceived to have a good work ethic is very important to him because he had such an intense reaction when someone implied that he's not seen that way.

For some people, verbally snapping at somebody could be considered *bad* or even *childish*. However, that reaction was what Junior's mind saw as the quickest way to stop the bad feeling (the negative emotion of anger). In Junior's repertoire, snapping at Senior seemed like the best method for achieving the highest positive intention of stopping the attack and restoring the perception of being a good employee. Now, although the angry outburst was not the best way to deal with things, its original intention - self-preservation of his personal identity - is still important.

Once you recognize the intended higher purpose of a negative emotion, you can then learn to separate the unpleasant feeling you experience from its *Higher Positive Intent*. This will then allow you to acknowledge the higher intention without being controlled by the overwhelming negative emotion. In this way you can choose how you want to meet the highest positive intent and, by doing so, still let go of all the bad feelings created by the whole situation.

FUNDAMENTAL LESSONS & LEARNINGS…

- The unconscious mind generates negative emotions when someone or something is in conflict with our deeper values and beliefs.
- Negative emotions are spotlights which highlight an experience or situation you need to deal with.
- Your reaction to bullying is what your mind thinks is the best way to stop the negative emotion and restore good feelings. However, being bullied by those negative emotions can often lead to bad decisions with short-lived success.

A Sense of Safety in Knowing

"Being defeated is often only a temporary condition. Giving up is what makes it permanent."
Marilyn vos Savant

Someone swings their fist and you duck. A vase falls off the top shelf and you jump to the side. You pull your hand off a hot stove. You decide at the last moment that maybe jumping out of a perfectly good airplane isn't such a smart idea, even with a parachute. Or, perhaps you get bullied at work so you buy a book on how to beat it.

Every living creature on Earth - including humans - has the instinctual drive for self-preservation. This means that it's automatic for us to want to be kept safe from any kind of harm - physical, mental and emotional. Thus, pain and fear are our biggest motivators at this level. Pain causes discomfort so we are driven to make that pain stop. Fear makes us want to seek situations of predictable safety.

Why is this important to know? Well, for all humans there are five basic needs and of those five the one that outweighs them all is the need for 'Safety, Survival and Self-Preservation'. If you perceive that your safety is at risk then it's difficult (if not impossible) to get any of your other needs met - meaning life is miserable unless you feel safe.

Humans have an instinctual drive for Self-Preservation; this means that it's automatic to want to feel safe.

Today it has become widely recognized that this instinctual need to feel safe is so important to all humans that, in our society, it is considered to be a 'Universal Right'. In fact, it is even included in the *United Nations Universal Declaration of Human Rights.*

FOR FURTHER CLARIFICATION...

SAFETY, SURVIVAL AND SELF-PRESERVATION

American psychiatrist, Dr. William Glasser is the developer of Reality Therapy and Choice Theory which focuses on personal choice, personal responsibility and personal control. One of the foundational components of Glasser's theories is the idea that people all have *5 Basic Needs,* consisting of; Safety, Survival and Self-Preservation; Love and Belonging; "ower; Freedom; and Fun. Of these five basic needs, the only one which holds sway over all the others is the need for Safety, Survival and Self-Preservation.

These needs mainly revolve around food, shelter and survival of our species which include things such as personal safety, health & wellness and hormonal sexuality. Our animal instincts, such as the human stress responses of freeze, flight, fight and fright, are all driven by these needs. In our modern society this category of safety and survival also incorporates our sense of risk taking, financial security and stability of predictable daily routines.

> ***You have both the right and the freedom to use Verbal Self Defense in order to stay safe.***

It's important to be aware that the original basic need for a sense of safety applies to our physical well-being as well as our mental and emotional wellness. In this way we are able to recognize that our *Universal Right to Personal Safety and Survival in this World* includes our mental and emotional wellness. This means that you have both the freedom and the right in our society to use verbal self defense whenever you feel mentally or emotionally attacked.

Let's just take a moment to make sure that last statement is absolutely clear.

FOR FURTHER CLARIFICATION...

ALWAYS REMEMBER

"Every person has the Universal Human Right to freely use Verbal Self Defense in order to maintain their mental and emotional health and wellbeing."

Dr. Daniel Scott, Msc.D.

Now, anytime you are verbally defending yourself and someone asks what gives you the right, simply quote the statement above and say, "Yes. Really, it's true... I read it in a book somewhere."

In the end, understanding that your need for basic safety and survival is motivating your actions will be helpful in choosing how you use the skills of verbal self defense. And therein lies the next key component - choosing. Your mind is already hard-wired for self-preservation so it's going to react and just 'do something' whether you want it to or not. Furthermore, you need to remember that your reaction will be whatever your unconscious mind deems the best immediate response for a quick solution, which may result in very undesirable long term consequences.

Even though we logically know the situation may not literally put our physical sense of safety at risk, when we are being bullied it's common to feel bad about it for days, if not weeks, afterwards. In some cases people ruminate for years about something that happened, wishing they could go back and change it. Logically we believe we are safe but emotionally we are not, and our mind unconsciously knows this. So, when we are bullied, our mind senses a form of danger and it instinctually wants us to successfully defend ourselves. This means it will use anything and everything it can to make that happen.

Now at this point our conscious awareness may prefer to do something appropriate and professional. In order to stop our unconscious mind from reacting without our control we can train ourselves to recognize this basic instinctual need for safety and use it as a trigger for decisive use of verbal self defense.

That is one of the first skills we are going to cover in this book but, like any good journey, the first thing we need is to know the destination. So, let us start by getting a clear picture of what you want your verbal self defense skills and abilities to look like by the end of this book.

DEVELOPING YOUR SKILLS & ABILITIES…

BECOMING A VERBAL DEFENDER

No two people will use verbal self defense the same way, so in order to become a good verbal defender you need to recognize your own strengths and weaknesses. This will allow you to know what you can build on and what you need to work to improve. Now, to do this properly it's best to know what you want and create a clear plan of how you expect to get it.

The easiest journeys always start with a clear destination, because if you have nowhere to go then you may end up going nowhere. In other words, if you don't know what you want to learn from this book you may end up not learning anything.

Since you want to reach a specific outcome you need to first know what that is, and what it is not. The following questions will help your mind (both conscious and unconscious) get a better idea of where you're headed. To make it more effective I strongly suggest you write your answers in point-form on a sheet of paper. Doing it this way frees your mind from trying to remember all the different skills and abilities you are hoping to build along the way.

What Don't You Want? You purchased this book with an intention, and that means there is something you hope to get from it. To ensure you get what you want you must know what that looks like; but, in order to know what this is, it's useful to start by clarifying the problem you're looking to overcome. Begin by making a list of recent experiences you've had where you wish you had known verbal self defense.

What Do You Want? Now, based on the list of unpleasant experiences you wrote down in answer to the question above, what do you wish was different about them? What do you wish you could have done differently in those situations? How specifically would you have like to have handled those interactions differently? Do you have a picture in your head of how you wish you could deal with people like that? Where the previous answer was about what you 'don't want,' this time define what you 'do want' instead?

What Are You Doing Now? Since you've thought about what you don't want and what you do want, the question now is: what have you been doing so far? It's time to define the reality of the current situation. What is or isn't happening? What do you do when dealing with similar circumstances? Consider how you have been handling situations like these up until now.

How Well Has That Worked So Far? Take a moment to really think about what you have been doing so far in order to get what you want. Has it been working? Is what you are doing getting you the outcome you want? Have you had any success so far and, if so, what was it and how did you get it?

When thinking about what is not working, get clear about what specifically you have been trying in order to change things. In the same sense, make a point to identify the things you are doing that are not gaining you anything!

What Do You Want To Do Differently? Now it's time

to look at other options. Start by listing the things that you want to be able to do that you have not been doing up to now. Be specific about how you'd like to feel and act. What do you want to be able to say or do in these kinds of events? Focus on the words and actions you need to change in order to get the outcome you want. In comparison, avoid getting caught up in wishing you could change how the other person thinks and behaves - only make note of things that you can directly do or say.

As you work toward becoming a verbal defender I think it's important to point out that this is a process of personal transformation. As we build on this you are going to discover new insights about what is important to you and what you are truly capable of.

As you move through this book you will move out of the shadow of uncertainty and doubt, and your sense of control over yourself and the world around you will become stronger. In the end, be prepared for the possibility that the general outcome you have written now may shift and change to become clearer as well as more self-initiated and self-maintained.

FUNDAMENTAL LESSONS & LEARNINGS…

- Your instinctual need for self-preservation gives you the right to use verbal self defense to ensure your mental as well as your emotional health and wellbeing.
- The instinct for safety and survival can be used to your advantage once you learn to control your unconscious reactions to situations of bullying - specifically by utilizing it as a trigger for verbal self defense.

THE BRAIN OF YOUR EXISTENCE

"Control yourself and you control the world around you."
Samurai Proverb

So now that you're beginning to define what workplace bullying looks like for you, we're going to need to start outlining why you feel the need to defend yourself, or more precisely, what it is you're defending. Before we can do that there is one more skill you need before you take your first step on the journey towards becoming a Master of Verbal Self Defense (in memory of all the good old kung-fu films, *cue the sound of wind chimes in the background*).

Okay… I realize that I'm talking about this stuff as if it were some kind of mystical martial art journey, and that may seem a bit cliché. In the literal sense you might be asking, "Sure… and where are we really going? It's not like I'm actually going to get up and take the book someplace special in order to learn verbal self defense."

Well, that's a good point and to answer it there is something important you need to understand: I'm not the one feeling bullied and so this isn't my journey - it's yours. At this point you might ask, "What kind of journey is it?" and the answer is: "It's one of learning." (Yes, I know how corny that sounds but it's still true.)

With that being the case, we all know that learning takes place in the mind, which means this book is going to be a journey through the lessons and learnings inherent in your own mind. I mean, there's no point in me telling you exactly what to say in certain situations - if I tried to tell you what to say and when to say it, well, there is no way I can cover every possible situation that could arise.

In the same way, there is no possible way to find one assertive statement that every single person reading this book would agree on as the best response. Thus, this book is NOT written that way.

> ***A good verbal defender must have an ability to be mindful of what they are doing.***

It's your life, so it has to be about your circumstances and your choice of words. That's what this book is going to teach you - how to incorporate your own way of thinking and your natural way of acting, or interacting, with your personal way of speaking to effectively apply defensive verbal tactics.

To do that, however, the first thing you must be able to do is focus your mind on each exercise as you learn it. In order to be the best verbal defender you possibly can be, you must develop an ability to be *mindful* of exactly what you're doing.

YOUR LIFE LIVES WITHIN YOUR MIND

Imagine two friends go to the same picnic. One comes back raving about the sunshine, great food and activities while the other has stories about the wind, the bugs and sand in his shorts. Based solely upon their descriptions it may sound like they didn't go to the same picnic. The reason is that from the moment a person is born we have all been gathering information and experiences that are unique to each individual.

Each and every moment you have lived, all that information has been taken in and sorted by your brain. All those experiences lead to the learnings, knowledge and understanding you have now of how the world works. To simplify it even further: lessons are when Event A happens then Outcome B is the result, where B is your reaction or experience.

So, each time a child experiences something for the first time it adds to their lessons and learnings, which are imprinted in their mind. After the same event leading to the same outcome occurs several times it becomes a kind of belief that it will happen like that *every* time. Basically when something happens 1 time it's interesting, 2 times is a coincidence but 3 times and your unconscious mind will consider it a pattern.

Combining everything that we are taught with all these experiences growing up each of us comes to develop our own personal set of Values and Beliefs about the world. These are all the things that we 'absolutely know' to be true or false, and right or wrong.

IMAGINE...

Max and Lucy are 1 year old toddlers and their parents have taken them to the park. The kids are toddling about under their parents' watchful eyes when a big, furry dog comes sauntering up, wagging its tail.

Max and Lucy stop, wide-eyed, about 6 feet away, amazed by this large, soft-looking beast. The dog's owner is there, holding the other end of the leash, and the big dog lets out a loud, "WOOF," which startles little Max and Lucy causing them to lean back and fall unceremoniously onto their (what we hope are still fresh) diaper-covered bottoms.

This is where Max and Lucy get to learn how to react to a big dog barking.

FAMILY (A): Max looks over at his parents with that, "Am I ok?" look. His parents run over, looking panicked, swoop in to gather him in their arms all the while saying, "There, there. It's okay. We won't let the big, mean doggie get you."

Perhaps they might even throw in a bit of barking themselves - berating the owner for letting such a large beast near their small child.

FAMILY (B): Lucy looks over at her parents with that same, "Am I ok?" look. Her parents calmly walk over and crouch down with smiling faces, speak with the owner in a friendly voice and ask if it's okay to pet the dog. Then they pet the dog and invite Lucy to do the same if she feels ready.

Neither scenario is inherently wrong or right. Each one just is the way it is, and from them we can make some guesses about what they teach little Lucy and Max about how to react to big dogs in the future. To over-simplify it, Max learned that being around big dogs can be a frightening and upsetting experience, but Lucy learned that being around big dogs is a calm and pleasant experience.

THE FILTERS OF YOUR MIND

In our mind, every time we learn something, and every time it is reinforced, it creates a filter for our perceptions through which we assimilate future information. We are exposed to television, family interactions, social interactions, bumps, bruises, first jobs, first dates, school and the trials and tribulations of life. As you can imagine, by the time we are adults we have many, many experiences (commonly called *memories*) which we use to sort, shape and interpret all new incoming information. These become our unconscious Mental Filters of the world.

Our memories, personal values, beliefs, morals, principles, etc. all work together to filter reality and create our individual perception of an experience.

So, why does your mind create these filters? The reason is because at any given moment in time you are being barraged with billions of bits of information coming in through your five senses. Every second of every day, all day long, throughout your entire life your senses are sending information to your brain. All that information from everything around you includes things like: the number of windows in the room you're in; the texture of things you're holding; the number of books on the 3rd shelf down on the right; all the colors; all the sounds; everything touching your skin including the temperature of the air around you; tastes; sights; smells; etc.

Literally every tiny detail that you *could* be aware of, your unconscious mind is aware of. So, you can imagine the jumble in your head if you were conscious of all these things at once! It would create such sensory overload that your brain would literally shut down from over-stimulation and you would pass-out.

This is one major reason your brain creates these filters. Your filters are kind of comparable to gatekeepers, silently rushing around in the background, deciding what you need to be aware of at any given moment in time. They tell you what is important at this second in time and they also help you figure out the meaning you will apply to that awareness. All your memories, personal values, beliefs, morals, principles, etc. work together to filter reality and create your individual perception of what is going on.

The challenge now comes when we are not fully aware, or *mindful*, of what our filters are doing. This is especially important when we have automatic reactions which are not always the best solution to the immediate problem.

IMAGINE…

Remember the Junior File Clerk from our earlier example. His unconscious filters (which were created from all his prior experiences of things like television, movies and seeing how others dealt with the same situation) told him, "Hey! This guy is totally insulting you! That hurts your feelings and makes you angry, so you need to strike back right away! Quick! Say something to hurt him just as much as he hurt you! Use this tone of voice and say…"

Although his mind was focused on achieving the highest positive intention of preserving his personal identity as a good employee, it did not filter the quarrel - or his choices of response - in the most beneficial way for dealing with the situation. Instead, his filters applied the fastest possible solution he could imagine for returning things to balance; he said something that would 'even the score'.

Taking Control of Your Mind

Now, it's important to remember that all this filtering happens unconsciously, in an instant. For most of us the majority of our personal perception (the unconscious filtering of the billions of bits of information coming in through our five senses) is outside our awareness and, consequently, outside our control. It is possible, however, for you to develop the ability to control your interpretation of that information.

The first step in controlling how you interpret your perceptions is being able to control your mind and focus on the parts of your perception which you choose rather than what your unconscious mind decides you need to pay attention to. This is where we come back to that challenge of being fully aware - being *mindful* - of what we are doing. To develop control over our awareness we use the process commonly referred to as *Mindfulness.*

For further clarification…

General Thoughts on Mindfulness

Mindfulness allows us to examine who we are and helps us clarify our view of the world.

Mindfulness is cultivating an appreciation for each moment.

Mindfulness is about being in touch with ourselves and the world around us.

Mindfulness means paying attention in a specific way - with purpose, in the present moment, and without judgment.

Mindfulness will nurture a greater awareness, clarity and acceptance of the reality of the present moment.

Mindfulness helps show us the way life unfolds in a procession of moments. If we are not present for many of these moments we may fail to realize the richness and the depth of our possibilities for growth.

Diminished awareness of the present moment will create problems through our unconscious, habitual responses.
These problems then build over time and can eventually leave us feeling stuck and without choice.

Mindfulness is a powerful tool for getting unstuck and increasing our awareness of options in the present moment.

Mindfulness is a way to take charge of the direction and quality of our life, starting right here and now.

A simplified explanation of mindfulness would be to say it's basically just paying attention to 'where you are' and 'what you are doing.' (Now put that sentence in Yoda's voice and you can imagine him saying it to Luke in the *Star Wars: Empire Strikes Back* movie.) This explanation can be simply translated into, "Consciously choosing to filter out distractions and direct your awareness toward what you choose".

I can hear your thoughts already, "Um... I know where I am and what I'm doing. I'm sitting here reading this book. I'm totally doing this 'mindfulness' thing already!" Well, yes and no: anyone can be mindful in times of relaxed contemplation. It's only through practicing the skills of mindfulness over a long period of time that you'll develop a greater ability to maintain control of your thoughts and emotions in a confrontational situation.

Using Verbal Self Defense without controlling your thoughts and perceptions is the same as physically defending yourself by wildly swinging your fists all around - it does not work. Only by controlling yourself can you control the situation.

Imagine...

> Let's consider the process of eating lunch, shall we? To be *intentionally aware* of eating lunch means we consciously take the time to notice the entire process of eating - deliberately taking note of all the sensations as well as our internal responses to those sensations.
>
> Try it. The next time you have something to eat ask yourself some questions during the process: How hot or cold is the food? Is it sweet, sour or salty? Is it dry and crunchy or soft and juicy? What do you smell? Do you hear crunching or squishing noises inside your head? Do you move the food back and forth in your mouth? Do you chew it on one side of your mouth or the other? What are you feeling in your body while you are eating? What facial expressions do you have? How does the cutlery feel in your hands? When you use the napkin, is it smooth and soft?
>
> Whenever you notice your mind beginning to wander off and think about other things - and let me assure you that it will happen even to people who've done this for years - when you find your mind wandering, intentionally bring your focus back to the task of eating. Avoid identifying your wandering mind as doing the *wrong* thing. Instead, simply recognize what's happening and turn your attention back to the process of eating.

This way of eating *mindfully* is completely opposite to the way people normally eat. Although we may be aware of what we are doing, we're usually thinking about other things at the same time, as well as watching TV, talking, or - God forbid - driving. Only a very small part of our awareness is used to attend to the process of eating so we barely notice any physical sensations and are even less aware of our feelings about those sensations.

Usually in the process of feeding ourselves we let our thoughts wander completely unrestricted with no conscious attempt to bring our focus back to eating. Left to itself, the mind can wander through all kinds of thoughts which might invoke feelings of anger, sadness, fear, shame, self-pity, etc. Only by consciously choosing what you want to focus your awareness on can you begin to develop a sense of control over where your mind goes. It does take practice but it's a skill anyone can develop. Now imagine: what other tasks do you do in a day where you can practice being mindful?

DEVELOPING YOUR SKILLS & ABILITIES...

EXERCISING YOUR MIND-FULNESS

Mindfulness can be compared to a lifestyle of participating in experiences with awareness as a way to live in the moment. With this in mind, there are three parts involved in being mindful: Observing, Describing and Participating.

These three components are explained in more detail. Read each one and then begin by practicing them separately. Start with Observing and practice it 3 times a day for a week. Then add the step of Describing by first observing and then describing an experience. Do this 3 times a day for a week. Finally, add the last step of Participating and consciously do this entire process of observing, describing and participating 3 times a day for a week.

When first learning to be mindful it's useful to stop and do each step by itself. You will find they eventually meld together into a single action - being mindful. Even so, it's too difficult to be mindful all the time, so until it's an unconscious habit start by choosing the times when you want to practice being mindful (i.e. showering, eating, washing dishes, etc.).

STEP 1: OBSERVING. Everyone has their own set of filters based upon what they have experienced in life up to the current moment in time. This means everyone has their own personal perception of what they see and feel. If we are not fully aware of things, our filters will automatically assign meaning to (and by extension, our automatic reaction to) what we experience.

The first step in learning to control how we consciously interpret each passing moment is to simply stop and take note of what you are experiencing:

- Be aware of what is happening around you without letting your mind get caught up in its own processes; experience something without reacting to your experience.

- Work to develop a *Teflon™ Mind* where things don't stick, but rather they simply slip past. As experiences, feelings and thoughts come into your mind just notice them and then allow them to go without dwelling on them.
- Control your attention without trying to control the event. Avoid focusing on any one thing and instead be open to an awareness of anything and everything as it comes to you.
- Imagine your consciousness is like a guard at the gate to your inner mind. Simply be alert to every thought, feeling and action that comes through the gate of your mind without questioning, labeling or stopping to inspect the awareness you experience.
- Be aware of what comes through each of your senses - what exactly your eyes see, your ears hear, your nose smells, your skin feels and your tongue tastes. Notice these things and, at this point, try to avoid putting words or descriptions to them.
- Be aware of people around you and their actions and expressions free of any labels or judgments.
- When memories come to mind turn your observation inward. Notice your thoughts coming and going like a leaf on the wind. Be aware of each feeling as it rises up and then recedes, like waves on the shore, rolling in and then rolling back out unimpeded.

Here is my example of Observing: *I am at my desk and I am aware there is something to the right of my computer within arm's reach. It is sitting on my desk and it has been there for about 15 minutes.*

Step 2: Describing. The second step in learning to be mindful is putting descriptions to the things you observe. When describing something it's important to remember that you are only focusing on the facts; no interpretation of any deeper or implied meanings. So, a frown is simply a frown and it does not necessarily mean the person is *sad* or *unhappy* or anything else.

- Begin describing your experiences. When a feeling

comes up, a thought comes to mind, or you do something, acknowledge it. For example, if you notice yourself experiencing anxiety say in your mind, "I'm now feeling anxious," or if you become aware of an uneasy feeling in your stomach say in your mind, "My stomach muscles are tingling," or if you think you cannot do something say in your mind, "The thought 'I can't do this' entered my mind."

- When you are experiencing an event put it into words. In your mind describe to yourself what is happening - label each feeling, notice every sensation, and take note of every sight and every sound. Identify a thought as a thought and a feeling as just a feeling. Avoid getting caught up in the content of what is happening; just describe it.
- When identifying feelings and emotions, start by simply noticing if the feeling is positive or negative. Then, explain the sensations that go along with the feeling and give the feeling a label such as fear, anger, frustration, etc.
- Avoid applying any judgments such as good and bad, or right and wrong.
- Be witness to only the facts of what you experience. Specifically be aware of what you see, hear, feel, taste, smell and think, without giving any interpretations or explanations.
- Pretend that someone has never experienced this before and they are not there to experience it with you right now. How would you describe it to them so they get an accurate understanding of what is happening and/or of what you are experiencing?

My example of Describing is: *The object I observed is about 4 inches high. It's white. Both the top and bottom are round and the whole thing is like a cylinder. It looks shiny.*

There is something sticking out of the side of it that looks like a hollow semi-circle. The top round part does not have a covering so it is open. I cannot see the bottom from this point of view. The whole object is hard and smooth to the touch. It's also warm. No sound is coming from this object and it does not move on its own.

There is something blackish in color inside it, and when the desk is bumped the blackish contents rippled in response as if it's a liquid. There's also steam rising from the liquid.

This liquid has a smell, which is acrid but sweet to me. My mouth feels dry and I feel tired. Looking at this object with the liquid in it gives me a feeling of hope that if I use it, my ability to do my task of writing will last longer.

Step 3: Participating. The final step in developing your mindfulness skills is learning to interact with your experiences without letting those experiences control your reaction(s). Put your mind into being a part of each moment, allow the previous moment to pass into the past, and choose what part of your immediate experience in the now you want to focus on. Take back control of that decision and choose to be present mentally, as well as physically.

- Join in with your experiences. Allow yourself to get involved in the moment, let go of ruminating and actively participate in the current situation.
- As you become part of the event, let go of your self-awareness and become one with the moment. Be a part of the experience (just another component of everything that is happening) with no awareness of anything else.
- Act intuitively with an open mind and do only what is needed in each situation. Like a dancer moving to the rhythm of the music, allow your experiences in the event to guide your actions.
- Focus experiencing just one moment at a time. Avoid letting your mind get caught on things that have already happened or on things yet to come.
- Participate fully in the experience of each moment with all your attention, awareness and focus.

For me, the example of Participating is: *I now know that this blackish liquid in the cylinder shaped thing on my desk is what I call coffee in a cup.*

> *I decide that now is a good time to drink it, so I reach out with my left hand, pick it up by holding the thing on the side I call the handle. Keeping it upright, I bring the closest edge to my lips, place my bottom lip on the outside of the rim, breathe in its aroma and slowly tip the cup so that the coffee gets closer to my top lip.*
>
> *As I gauge the temperature of the coffee while it is getting closer and closer to my lip, I determine it is not too hot and so I proceed. Allowing the liquid to enter my mouth until I have enough, then closing my lips I swallow the mouthful of coffee as I return the coffee mug to its upright position, pull it away from my mouth and return it, still in its upright position, to its original spot on the desk.*
>
> *Feeling the solid resistance of the desk as the cup reaches its original place on the desk, I believe it will stay there without tipping over. Finally I let go of the handle and pull my hand back.*

Now, I recognize you are probably thinking, "WTF! You want me to take time to … uh … what? Think about all these things … how?"

Remember, this is simply an exercise to help strengthen your mental control. This is merely mindfulness training where you practice maintaining a strong degree of control over your awareness. In an actual verbal self defense situation you will not actually do mindfulness to this extreme, but rather, you will notice your mind is clearer and you will be less likely to get caught off guard or lose focus.

A person trying to use verbal self defense without maintaining control of their perceptions and thoughts is equivalent to a person physically defending themselves by wildly swinging their fists in every direction - it is inefficient and ineffective. Only by having control of yourself and your mind will you be able to control the situation. Mindfulness training is practicing the self-control you need by taking it to an extreme. So - in answer to your question - "Yes, you should practice this exercise to this degree." Choose small situations and little events where you can practice being as mindful as possible. Do it 3 times a day for a week and your ability to focus and concentrate will improve greatly.

FUNDAMENTAL LESSONS & LEARNINGS…

- Everyone has their own set of filters which are created from what that person has experienced in life up to now. This also means that everyone has their own personal perception of an experience and it will be different from everybody else's.
- If you're not fully aware of your surroundings, your internal filters will automatically decide what you will pay attention to and assign meaning to it. Then your unconscious mind will generate your reaction to the situation based upon that meaning.
- The first step in learning control over how we consciously interpret all the information coming through our filters is to practice *mindfulness*.

PART II

Get Out of My Shoes

When you're growing up life is full of learning; everything is all new and exciting through the eyes of a child. Each experience is foreign and strange to us the first time it happens but, from then on that original experience becomes a sort of mental reference which we use as a comparison for our future experiences.

In fact, you actually use the combination of all your past experiences as a way to identify, understand and explain the things that are happening in the present moment. Your perceptions about whatever you're experiencing right now are all based on what you've experienced throughout your life and the lessons you learned from those experiences. Even the way you imagine events happening in the future are based on your past experiences.

These memories from your past - which you compare current events to in order to understand what's going on - are referred to in NLP as your *Referential Experiences* because they are the previous 'experiences' you use as a 'reference' in order to explain what you perceive to be happening now. Some of these referential experiences are either repeated often enough or had such a significant reward/consequence that we personally put more value on them. These types of experiences become a generalized set of standard expectations which we use as our guidelines for understanding and relating to the world around us.

People often put a very high value on the lessons and learnings they gain from those types of significant events. In fact, the *rules* we create in order to define how life is supposed to work are all derived from the wisdoms gained through those kinds of experiences.

This is what most people refer to as their particular version of *Common Sense* (which they assume everyone knows as well). Eventually a person can even go so far as to say those common sense learnings are so important that they actually become part of that person's deep personal values, beliefs, principles and morals.

IMAGINE...

Each time young Sally stuck her tongue out at people her mom would yell at her. Eventually, the bad feeling Sally got each time she stuck her tongue out created a connection between the two - sticking your tongue out is equal to feeling bad. The basic lesson she learned was: sticking your tongue out at people is bad.

Years later, as an adult, Bob and Sally are co-workers and one day he playfully sticks his tongue out at her as a joke. Bob and his dad did it as a kind of childhood game and so Bob learned the lesson that: sticking your tongue out at people is silly and fun.

However, rather than laughing, Sally becomes very offended by his action. Since Bob never had Sally's experience growing up, and it was something she has never felt the need to explain to him, then it can be difficult for Bob to understand why Sally is taking his playful behavior as offensive.

For Sally it's common sense that sticking your tongue out is *mean and hurtful*, and to Bob it's common sense that sticking your tongue out is *just being silly*. Now, notice how they're both right based on their own personal referential experience.

This natural use of past referential experiences to define the meaning and understanding of life experiences applies to not only other people's behaviors but to everything we know and believe about the world. We use our referential experiences to explain our understanding of objects, events, people, places, skills, decisions, etc. Referential experiences are what help us remember that the sky is blue, water is wet, and gravity makes things that go up come down.

In the same way that we use our prior experiences of external events to understand the things happening around us, we also use our prior experiences of interpersonal communication with others to learn how to communicate with people. A teacher or parent will show a toddler a cup and say the word, "Cup". If the toddler experiences that same thing enough times it comes to the conclusion that the word *cup* is the same as the object.

Going one step further, in the early years of learning when we all experience events which incorporate interactions with other people, we take the experience of those events and use them to define the 'right and wrong' way to interact with others - such as how to properly use our tone of voice, etc.

Relating to Other Peoples' Experiences

Many of us have heard about the *Golden Rule,* which says: "Do unto others as you'd have done unto you". The general idea behind the Golden Rule is that a person should treat other people the way they themselves want those people to treat them. This is a guiding principle common in cultures and communities around the world and it's usually taught as a way to learn tolerance and/or empathy.

When a parent wants to explain the golden rule they are often heard asking their child a questions like, "How do you think they felt when you did that?" or, "How would you feel if someone did that to you?" The intention of questions such as these is to get a child to imagine experiencing the same event from the other person's point of view.

At first, this tactic for teaching how to be more considerate of others will definitely help them develop an ability to be empathetic and sympathetic. However, if we do something and experience the same outcome enough times, eventually we come to the conclusion that this is how it will 'always' be every time we do it in the future (for ever and ever and ever and ever). In time, we start to use the accumulation of our past referential experiences as a way to set certain expectations of how to predict outcomes of future experiences. An example is, if you try eating mushrooms and each time you are disgusted by the taste then eventually you begin to predict that you will hate mushrooms if you try them again. However, the truth is that people's tastes change over time and, although you hated mushrooms in the past, it's possible that you may like mushrooms now.

In regard to interpersonal communication, let's say we consider someone's body language and facial expression when determining what they are feeling and - having interpreted their non-verbal cues correctly - it helps us be more effective in the way we interact with that person. If we do this enough times and every time we are right in how we interpret someone's non-verbal communication, then eventually the way we interpret those particular non-verbal cues becomes ingrained as a habitual response.

One main goal is to separate out your own perceptions, thoughts and feelings from what you think the other people might be perceiving, thinking and feeling.

After a while, each time you empathize with someone and you are correct in interpreting what they are feeling, it merely confirms that you no longer need to ask them. You eventually lose your curiosity about identifying what emotion the other person might be feeling based on the way they are acting. Instead you simply start applying meaning to other people's words and behaviors and eventually it leads to assuming you are able to know how others feel.

As we get older, the meaning we learn to apply to certain facial expressions, body posture, tone of voice, etc. becomes so automated at an unconscious level that we reach a tipping-point where we become inflexible in how we interpret and understand others' non-verbal cues. Eventually we start believing that whatever we assume others are thinking and feeling is absolutely correct and without question. Our over-confidence can be so strong that when someone tries to assert anything different than our interpretation we simply discount their arguments with explanation like, "They don't understand what I mean."

In verbal self defense our goal is to return to a purer model for understanding others by simply identifying what behaviors we are aware of and then clarify whether or not our interpretation is correct. This is a great way to avoid taking things personally (unjustly applying negative meaning to someone's communication) while still remaining open to understanding them. The result is that we will be much more effective at dealing with a situation, instead of just reacting to it.

WELL I THINK...

"Be independent of the good opinion of others."
Wayne Dyer

A gentleman by the name of Gregory Bateson was the first to define the words used to describe the fundamental characteristics of a relationship as *Characterological Adjectives*. The main idea with characterological adjectives is that when you define one side of the relationship, you automatically imply the other side of that same relationship. So, if someone is the victim in a relationship then that means the other person must be the perpetrator.

When we apply Bateson's concept of characterological adjectives to verbal self defense it means that when you are defensive in your communication with another person, then there must be some form of aggression on the part of the other person. This natural way of defining a relationship directly affects how your mind filters what they say and how they say it. If you expect someone to be aggressive then you will unconsciously apply that meaning to any components of their communication such as their body posture, facial expression or tone of voice in order to prove your perceptions are correct.

IMAGINE...

> As a simple example, if Jane believes her boss is always criticizing her then when the boss asks, "What are you doing?" Jane might think: "Obviously his tone of voice really means he's saying, 'You're doing it wrong!'"
>
> In reality he may actually just be curious to see if she's ready to go to lunch. Since Jane has already made up her mind as to what the underlying meaning is, even if he explains himself she'll simply discount his explanation by telling herself, "He just doesn't want to admit that he doesn't like the way I've decided to do it".

Your goal as a verbal defender is to learn how to control the way you filter your perceptions so that you can differentiate between how the other person is really acting and the way you perceive the experience. Learning this skill will allow you to filter out the unconscious meaning that your mind automatically applies to someone's communication and you can stop your mind from creating assumptions about any hidden or implied meaning you think a person's words and actions might have. Specifically, it's the key to stop any unconscious filters that are *looking for bullying behaviors* when you're dealing with an office bully.

Whenever you let your mind make assumptions about a possible underlying message behind the way a person talks to you, then you automatically communicate with them believing that they are already thinking those assumed underlying messages. By stopping that unconscious habit it will reduce the chance for miscommunication and misunderstandings.

Instead, by using your ability to recognize the way you're filtering someone's communication you will have greater control over the message you send. This allows you to ensure your actual communication is more aligned with your intended message (just because the other person is yelling doesn't mean you need to yell too, especially if you want to send the message that this situation can be resolved calmly).

This higher degree of control will give you a greater amount of choice in determining the best way to communicate with a person (tone, words, body language, etc.). This will make you more effective at getting them to understand what you are really trying to explain instead of them incorrectly filtering your communication.

In the end you will have the ability to send a message based on your actual experience of the interaction without incorporating any implied messages that you unconsciously think are hidden in the other person's non-verbal cues. This means, fewer hurt feelings, fewer misunderstandings, less sitting around after work getting angry at yourself thinking, "What I should have said was…"

Filtering Out the Filters of Others

When we're alone and thinking about the things we see, or hear, or read, or feel, it's easy enough for most of us to decide what we personally believe about each experience. If we add other people into the situation (especially people who are significantly important to us) then it starts to influence the way we will perceive those same events. The more people we keep adding, or the more important those people are to us, then the more and more our thoughts and feelings are influenced by those around us; the mere presence of other people will adjust how we filter events in our life.

> ***It is better to know what you believe and choose to be silent, than it is to simply react using other people's opinions.***

IMAGINE...

Let's consider a simple experience of reading an article in the newspaper. If it's a general news issue about the world beyond your own community, then you can consider what you read and form your own opinion (or perception) of the information provided without too much concern about how it relates to other people's opinions.

Alternatively, when the news article is more personal, such as when it relates directly to your own community or your personal family specifically, then you will feel a greater connection to it, and consequently have more significant thoughts and feelings towards the content. Healthcare is a good example of a topic commonly considered to be more controversial for people because if affects all of us at some level.

Furthermore, the more directly related the current discussion is to your personal livelihood, the stronger your individual reaction will be to it. This can sometimes be partly due to past referential experiences such as your family having always been a strong supporter of a certain point of view.

Let's say a fellow named George grew up in a home environment where the people he looked up to were always spouting praise for Political Party A, saying they are *the best*. It's likely George will grow up believing the same thing and eventually become a strong supporter of Political Party A.

Now, at this point let's add another person to the mix and see what could happen:

SITUATION 1: Imagine George is talking with someone about a news article regarding Political Party A and the other person has a very strong opinion against Party A, saying they are *the worst*. If this opponent is someone George doesn't know, such as a stranger at a bus stop, he may or may not feel the need to assert his political opinion. If George is the type of person who believes politics is a very important issue he could get upset and begin presenting arguments which conflict with the stranger's perceptions, even if all he does is repeat things that his family told him growing up.

SITUATION 2: For comparison, let's change the stranger in the previous situation to be someone George has a stronger connection to, such as his employer. If George feels that expressing his opinion (which is in direct conflict with his boss's) is going to make his boss upset with him then he might choose to avoid asserting his political point of view. George may go so far as to outwardly act as if he agrees with his boss, mimicking the boss's opinion; nodding when the boss nods; showing anger or disgust at issues the boss shows anger or disgust with; etc. However, in his own mind George might be very aware of what specifically about the boss's comments he believes to be true or untrue based on his own personal experiences.

In *Situation 1* it seems like George was asserting his own point of view, but he was not. Instead George was simply repeating the arguments he had heard from his family when growing up. In short, he was asserting his family's point of view, not his own.

In *Situation 2* George may be outwardly pretending to take on his boss's point of view, however, the truth is George remained very in-touch with his true feelings about what he believes to be right and wrong. Although he was not technically asserting his opinions George was very clear about what they were.

In the second situation George consciously decided that it was going to be much more valuable for him to silently maintain his own point of view, compared to the first situation where he simply reacted using other people's thoughts and beliefs without understanding why.

Whenever you're considering an experience from your own point of view it's important to remember that it should only incorporate your own personal perceptions of the situation or event. All communication you experience should be only from your own perspective seeing just what you see; hearing exactly what you hear; feeling only what your body is telling you. Anything you imagine from someone else's point of view could change your perceptions in ways you don't understand and, consequently, can't verbally defend.

CLARIFYING YOUR OWN PERCEPTIONS

Whenever you are filtering things in order to clarify your own point of view you should take note of everything that is happening around and inside you, but avoid applying meaning to anything you see, hear and feel. Be mindful of your point of view without allowing it to control your reaction. If you see a person's eyebrows furrow you could ask if it's a sign they might be angry, but remember that it does not necessarily mean they are angry at you! Applying unconfirmed interpretations to your perceptions will only lead to further misunderstandings and miscommunications.

If you feel it's appropriate to label or judge some of the communication you experience then recognize it as your label for that experience based only on your perception in that moment. This means that if you experience something abusive then avoid assuming that the other person perceives the same thing in the same way. In reverse, avoid assuming that other people see things the same as you - just because you think you're treating someone in a good way doesn't mean they have the same perception of your behavior as you do.

DEVELOPING YOUR SKILLS & ABILITIES...

FILTERING FOR YOUR OWN POINT OF VIEW

Learning to be more aware of and pay more attention to your own personal point of view is a valuable tool for any communicator. It's that special little skill which allows you to identify what, specifically, you need or want from someone, and what you are willing to do in order to get it.

We all have expectations in life but sometimes we just

do not recognize them until we are not getting them. Yes, it's true that when you're alone it's easier to fully delve into your own awareness and really connect with who you are and what you feel. However, there are probably very few situations where you'll require verbal self defense when you are completely alone.

So, to effectively connect with your own point of view properly while being in conflict with another person you will need to disconnect from the other people involved. In order to do this it's necessary to watch their actions and behaviors, listen to their words and tone of voice and take all that information in as just that - *information.*

This can be easily achieved by applying your mindfulness training as you watch and listen to the other person, without any judgment or expectation. What precisely do you hear them saying and how do you hear them saying it? What specifically do you see them doing?

By being mindful of the other person's communication and taking it in as 'just information' you will be better able to remain in contact with your own deeper values and beliefs. As well, it helps you avoid the risk of unconsciously mirroring it back to them and sending the wrong message.

All together this will give you the ability to stay in control of your communication and help guide you in making the choices that are more congruent with your underlying needs and intentions (which we'll look more closely at in the coming chapters). It also removes any power they would usually have over you, meaning they won't be able to 'push your buttons' because you can choose your response rather than automatically giving them the reaction they're looking for.

Each day for a week, for only a minute or two, practice your mindfulness during a conversation with a friend. Learn to avoid getting caught up in the emotions of the discussion and just perceive and interact without expectations.

Being properly rooted deep in your own perceptions means you'll be unable to objectively see yourself since everything you experience will be through your own senses. Subsequently you'll be unable to see your own facial expressions and non-verbal cues, however, you will have access to all your inner wisdom.

The benefit is that you'll be more aware of the deep values and beliefs that are guiding your decisions and filtering your understanding of the immediate situation. So, as you learn to experience an event while paying attention to your own perceptions it's important to always use words such as Me, Myself and I when referring to your own beliefs, experiences, ideas, feelings and point of view.

In the end it will be a bit of a trade off - you'll have greater awareness of your own thoughts and feelings (uncontaminated by other people's point of view), but you will sacrifice the ability to consider your communication through the external perceptions of the person you're talking to (which would effectively taint your own point of view if you try to do both simultaneously).

Developing your skills & abilities...

Improving Awareness of Your Experiences

The next time you have an argument or discussion with someone, when it's over, take some time to review the event in your mind. Remember what you were talking about and how it went. Think about the way it started, progressed and finally came to an end.

Now, rewind the memory to the beginning and go through the entire event in your mind from start to finish a few times in order to get a real sense of what you experienced. As you do, make sure you're experiencing everything from your own point of view - seeing what you saw, hearing what you heard, feeling what you felt, etc. Then, when you're ready, write out the following:

Describe the Event. How would you briefly describe the way you remember the event going? If you were to explain what happened in only a few sentences, what key points do you feel it's important to mention?

What They Said. What do you remember hearing the

other person say? Really try to recall exact words and phrases that you heard. Specifically, were there any particular phrases or comments they kept repeating? Just list out what you can remember in point form.

HOW THEY SAID IT. Often, *what* someone says is not as important as *how* they say it. If you truly want someone to understand how you perceived the event it's important to be able to explain the tone of voice you heard the other person use.

How would you describe the different tones of voice you heard the other person use when they were talking during your interaction? As much as possible try to avoid emotional labels such as angry - instead describe *how* they spoke using adjectives and adverbs such as low, deep, loud, fast etc.

HOW THEY ACTED. What kind of descriptors would you use to explain how the person behaved? Specifically, how would you describe their posture, the kind of facial expressions they used, or any notable movements or hand gestures they made?

WHAT YOU FELT. List out some of the things you felt during the event. Avoid summarizing your feelings as *emotions*, such as angry or frustrated. Instead describe what you actually felt in your body as you experienced the emotions.

For example, instead of *stressed* you might describe it as, "experiencing sensations of tension in your shoulders; clenching your jaw; feeling a weight on your chest; etc." - the physical sensations you experienced.

WHAT YOU THOUGHT. What were some thoughts you had during the discussion? Did you say anything to yourself inside your own mind as you were going through the interaction?

Make note of which thoughts you actually expressed and believe the other person understood. Are there any thoughts you tried to explain but think they didn't understand? Also, write down any thoughts you didn't even attempt to express at all.

Now take a few minutes to review everything you wrote down from the exercise above. Look for things that you assumed or presumed to be understood even though they were never actually said. As well, be certain it's all exactly what you 'actually' experienced without any interpretation or explanations.

Notice which of your words and behaviors were things you did or said consciously on purpose, and take note of which parts were simply reactions to something the other person said or did. It's useful to underline those parts that were simply an automatic reaction and make note of what you were reacting to. An example might be if you raised your tone of voice in response to them raising theirs.

After that, highlight the things you said, did, thought or felt 'on purpose'. What was your intention in doing or saying those things? Did they get the response you expected?

Keep this exercise in mind the next time you are talking with someone. It can be extremely enlightening when you begin to realize just how much of what you do and say are unconsciously created responses which you don't truly understand the purpose of. By focusing on any one of the points in this last exercise it's possible for you to develop your ability to be more aware of (and consequently have more control over) the way you interact with people.

FUNDAMENTAL LESSONS & LEARNINGS...

- By defining one side of a relationship you automatically imply the other side of that relationship - this will have a direct impact on how you filter that other person's communication.
- People naturally dislike being wrong - so if you believe someone is abusive then your unconscious mind will filter how you react/interact with them in order to try and get that person to behave in the abusive way you expect them to.
- The benefits of learning to filter your perception of other people's communication is that you have more control over your own communication, plus you are free from applying any negative meanings to the experiences (the unconscious process which usually leaves us feeling emotionally or mentally hurt).

I KNOW, YOU THINK ...

"We don't see the world as it is.
We see it as we are."
Anais Nin

The principle of *General Semantics* has been described as a 'general system of evaluation and awareness' - two components integral to verbal self defense. The founder of this principle, Alfred Korzybski, had a basic premise that, the map is not the territory.

Now, we've all seen maps before, right? Whether it's a map of the world, a country or even a city, you can easily see the difference is in the levels of detail. The problem is that no matter how detailed a map is, it always leaves something out. In comparison to the actual territory which, the map is designed to represent, the actual place leaves nothing out - everything that is there will be there (on a map or not).

The original concept that *the map is not the territory* was simply Korzybski's way of saying that, "the words we use are not the actual event or item they are intended to represent". This basic communication principle illustrates that each person's internal Mental Map of life's experiences is different from the actual experience itself. One's *mental map* is simply the internal representations of their perceptions. In comparison, the concept of the territory is equivalent to the actual external events, experiences, tangible objects, etc. which the person's internal representation is meant to correspond to.

Your own personal mental map is simply a way of referring to all the experiences stored in your memory. Out of these memories come all your personal values, beliefs and understandings about life. Yet, all of these experiences stored in your mind are simply *internal representations* of the original event which were created at the time you experienced them. In fact, that internal representation is actually based on the information that was left after the experience was filtered by your unconscious mind. If you think of it that way it means your memories are merely the pieces you remember of the actual external event when and where it happened.

Every single person has a different perception of what reality actually is.

Now, science has shown that at any given moment in time there are millions of bits of information being received through your five senses. However, a couple of guys by the names of Miller and Galanter discovered decades ago that of these millions of bits of information our mind filters each moment in time down to approximately 7, plus or minus 2, pieces of information. This result is that we build our internal representation of our experiences based on only 5 to 9 particular details which we received through our five senses at that moment. Thus, the likelihood of two people having the same perception of a single event becomes astronomical.

Ultimately this means that every single person has a different perception of what reality actually is, but nobody's mental map is any more real or true than any other because none of them will ever be the actual, external experience. As a Buddhist Monk once noted, "No matter how I explain watermelon to you, it will never be the same as when you go, get a watermelon, cut it open and take a bite of it yourself."

In the end, everyone's mental map is created from different bits of information taken from the expansive territory (which is the actual experiences in life). In the same way, the words we use to describe an experience are not the actual experience itself. Words, written or spoken, are merely symbols used to convey a message. They're a way to describe our inner perceptions and - considering how astronomical the odds are of two people having the same internal perception for a single event - it's just as unlikely two people will have the same meaning for a single word.

Together, all of this means that every other person in this world is behaving and communicating based upon their own inner mental map of how the world works... not yours. That simple observation allows you to recognize that your perceptions of a person's words or behaviors as being 'abusive' is most likely not the way the other person perceives it in their own mind. The solution then is to realize and accept that nobody's mental map (not even our own) is more true or real than someone else's - merely different.

IMAGINE...

Let's say one evening a young family decides to go out for dinner. After much deliberation they choose a recently opened restaurant boasting good food, great service and fun for the whole family.

Once the family arrives they quickly discover there will be a significant wait to get a table. Then, after finally getting their table the waitress is having difficulty keeping up with service and takes an unusually long time to serve them drinks and take their order. Being so rushed, when she brings their food out it is unceremoniously plunked on the table with little or no courtesy. Whisking away, she doesn't even give the family time to explain the mistakes that have been made with their orders.

A Generalized Courteous Reaction. Some people might feel it's best to simply accept the situation by acknowledging the recent opening of the restaurant as an explanation for the long waits, rushed service and simple errors. In an effort to be supportive of their server and the small business owner, the parents may forego correcting the errors with their food orders and encourage their children to make the best of a bad situation by enjoying the food they have (albeit mashed potatoes and gravy instead of fries and gravy) at least it's delicious food that has been well prepared.

Afterwards the family would probably leave the

restaurant without taking any time to make a complaint to the manager. They believe that doing so would only disrupt other people's dinner and perhaps leave everyone feeling uncomfortable for listening to someone's understandable grievances. All things being considered, other patrons may or may not have had just as poor an evening, however, it is certain that the next time this particular family thinks about dining out they will remember how terrible their experience was at the new restaurant and likely choose to eat elsewhere. The result is that the owner of the restaurant will never be able to fix the problems or make up for the poor service.

A Generalized Assertive Reaction. Other people might believe that it is more important to make the effort to fix what is not right. To show their children how to stand up for what they believe in and go after what they want, the parents politely call over the hostess and kindly explain the mix up in the orders and have the mistakes sent back to be fixed. When their meals finally arrive, they will all enjoy their food even though it took longer than expected.

Afterwards the couple might go so far as to speak with the manager and enlighten him to the poor quality of service due to long wait times and the rude behavior of the staff. Although the conversation is polite, it will still leave the nearby tables of patrons feeling a bit embarrassed for the manager who is getting in trouble. Since all these things delay the time before the family leaves the restaurant it means that someone else is waiting in line at the door even longer for their own table. So now, not only did this particular family have a less enjoyable evening, it's certain that several other people did too.

On the other hand, the manager can now address the problems and ensure that service improves so that future patrons will a have pleasant dining experience. As well, he has an opportunity to make up for their bad experience by offering to discount the family's meal, thus making them feel important and giving them reason to come back again in the future.

Whichever family you might relate better to, one thing to keep in mind is that there are dozens of factors which can influence whether a person chooses one way of dealing with this kind of situation or the other.

For the first family, they think that politely making the best of a bad situation is the best way to be considerate of others (the *others* being their fellow patrons). The second family showed how pointing out people's mistakes so they can correct them is the best way to be considerate of others (*others* in this case meaning the restaurant owner). One family believes people should simply endure and provide feedback through conventional means such as leaving a smaller tip or boycotting the small business. The other family believes that people should fight for what they want and take a stand even if it hurts someone's feelings.

Simplified, we can summarize it as, "You can go away feeling bad knowing that others feel okay in the short term, even if it might lead to them failing in the future. Or you can make someone feel bad so that they can improve and make things better in the long term." Neither is right and neither is wrong; it's simply two different ways of handling the same situation.

Comparing Mental Maps

Whenever humans let go of their ego-based need to prove they are right and other people are wrong, then the focus changes from defending their own mental map to learning and utilizing other peoples' mental maps in order to get them to understand what we are saying. This is the subtle difference between the idea of teaching someone a lesson and helping someone to understand.

An old way of teaching children how to relate better to someone else's mental map is to ask them to, "put themselves in the other person's position". The idea is to get the child to consider a situation from another person's point of view. This ultimately led to the infamous comment, "Well, if I were you, I would have…"

The problem with this phrase is that, if you were them, then you would have all their experiences, lessons, learning and understanding, so of course you would have made a different decision; however, the fact is that you are not them and you do not have their inner knowledge so you will not make the same choice(s) they would.

When a person chooses to say something or do something their decision has the unconscious intention to meet his or her deeper need at that time and in that situation. The guidelines that person uses to make their choice are based on their own individual values and beliefs.

Although it may be difficult to believe, every person is unconsciously trying to stay true to their own personal values. Ultimately each of us unconsciously wants to think of ourselves as a highly moral person. The key is remembering that each person's individual morals, values and beliefs are based upon their own mental map of how the world works (which we know is based upon their unique experiences throughout their life). This means that a person's perceptions of right and wrong are subjective based on what they learned in their life. An example of this has been seen in countries experiencing civil war, where kids will identify murder as wrong and unethical except when asked about killing someone for the purpose of revenge, in which case they identify murder as *an acceptable form of vengeance*.

Even in such extreme circumstances it doesn't matter what behavior a person exhibits, the basic premise remains that, based on all their past knowledge combined with their perception of the current situation, their present behavior is the best choice available to them in order to get their needs met. It's believed that if their mental map had the option of a better choice which would be just as effective for dealing with the situation, and still achieve their highest positive intention, then they would unconsciously choose to do that behavior instead.

To be as effective as possible at verbal self defense, you need to be able to consider the bully's point of view.

Combining this knowledge with the fact that every new experience throughout our lives is capable of altering one's mental map means that human behavior is actually geared for adaptation and is constantly changing. So, assuming that people are making the best choices available to them in the immediate moment and assuming that if they were aware of a more effective behavior for getting their needs met then they would choose it instead, this means your focus as a verbal defender can shift from convincing someone they are being a bully to focusing on bringing to their awareness a more useful (and less abusive) choice of behavior that will meet their needs. This way you can accept the person (and their mental map) while still taking care of your own mental and emotional safety by working towards changing their bullying behaviors.

At this point you should remember that, in order for you to bring to someone's attention a more useful option, you must be able to connect with and understand their mental map. When you can utilize internal representations unique to their way of understanding the world it becomes much easier to explain things in a way they can relate to. By communicating in this way you will quickly find you have a greater degree of control over a situation (*your level of flexibility*) and you'll be more effective at dealing with whatever type of workplace bullying you experience.

Exchanging Mental Maps

In order to be a truly effective verbal defender it's quite useful to consider where the other person is coming from. In order to do this properly you want to avoid applying your own way of thinking to their point of view and avoid using your own mental map to filter how you think they are experiencing the situation. When we habitually apply our own filters to another person's point of view it's equivalent to considering their experience *as if they were us*. That would basically imply that they would know what we're thinking; however the truth is *they don't*.

Instead, you want to consider the experience from their point of view only - what they see; what they hear; how they are moving; the gestures they are making; etc. In this way you can, firstly, get input about how effective your own communication actually is for the other person. Secondly, you'll be able to catch yourself when you make unconfirmed assumptions about what they already know.

Rather than pretending to read their mind and guess what they're thinking, it gives you the chance to ask for clarification whenever there is the possibility of any confusion. In the same way, you also become aware of what they do not know and what your message is and is not saying. This will allow you to adjust or add to your communication in order to be more effective.

Whenever you choose to consider another person's perspective it should be a mental process in which you imagine being in the other person's physical location, in their physical posture, making their physical gestures and generally experiencing the world through their 5 senses. Remember that, in your mind, it's extremely important to disconnect as much as possible from your own point of view and try to fully associate into the other person's perspective.

Imagine temporarily leaving all your own personal values, beliefs, memories and knowledge behind. Experience the event through their senses without any judgments, assumptions or expectations. As you briefly take on the other person's point of view in your mind you want to address yourself in the event as 'you' (as opposed to 'I' or 'me') using the language patterns of the person you are pretending to be.

After you've experienced another person's point of view it's just as important to return to yourself cleanly. Leave behind all the *values and beliefs* which you perceived from the experience of being them, in their position. Go back to being yourself, experiencing the world from your own point of view, taking with you the information you gathered from temporarily being in the other person's position. Using the new wisdom you received from taking their position you can then evaluate how effective your communication is. Ask yourself, "Am I expressing my message in the best way to get them to understand - using the right tone of voice, the most effective facial expression and the best body posture to express the message I want them to get?"

DEVELOPING YOUR SKILLS & ABILITIES …

GETTING ANOTHER PERSON'S POINT OF VIEW

GETTING THEIR *PERCEPTIONS.* As you practice taking on another person's point of view, always remember that the most important part of the process is suspending your own values and beliefs for the time you are pretending to experience the situation as the other person. This will allow you to better understand the way that person perceives your communication, without any of the pre-existing knowledge, beliefs or judgments you might assume they already have.

Once you are able to let go of all your assumptions, your expectations, everything you believe about how the interaction 'should' go, or to what degree things are apparently right or wrong, along with the things you think should be common sense, then you are ready to imagine the experience from the other person's position.

A good way to practice this is by thinking back to a recent interaction you had with someone (even something quick and simple such as a short conversation with a store clerk). Recall everything that took place and then go back to the beginning of the memory and imagine going through it again pretending to be the other person instead.

In your mind, imagine you perceive everything that is happening as if you were the other person. Mentally put yourself in their physical location and let go of any prior knowledge or experiences that you would normally have as yourself.

Using their posture, consider what you might be feeling - what would you physically sense? Which muscles would be relaxed and which would be tight? Imagine saying what they said using their tone of voice, with the same inflections. Take note of what you are actually saying and how you are saying it. Imagine making their facial expressions and hand gestures just as they did in the original event.

As you are doing all these things pay attention to anything you notice about what you might need to think or believe about the world in order to communicate this way. You know that every human being is making the best choice available at any given moment in time and every behavior has a higher positive intent - do you get a sense of theirs? It's interesting to wonder, "What would have needed to happen in this person's life that would leave them believing their current words and actions are absolutely the right thing to do?"

This means that, as you are pretending to be in the other person's point of view, the things you are saying and doing are *not* meant to be abusive. So, what do you perceive their intention could be as you mimic their words and actions? Being in their position, also notice what you're focusing on as you communicate with the other people in this situation? Remember that you are thinking about all this as you imagine yourself in the other person's point of view without any of your own knowledge, beliefs or values.

At this point let's also remember that communication is usually a two way interaction. That means that, while you are imagining being in the other person's point of view, you are not only communicating with others but you are also experiencing their communication with you. Even someone who is ignoring a person is still sending them a type of message (lack of interaction is still a form of communication).

Remaining in the other person's position (still free of any preconceptions or expectations) take the time to notice how everyone else is speaking and acting toward you, as you are pretending to be the other person. Pay special attention to the original 'You' in the event and how that person is communicating. What do you notice about their posture, facial expressions, tone of voice and gestures?

Now, take all the knowledge you got from being in the other person's point of view and - leaving behind any beliefs or values which you may have imagined in that position - shift back to your own original body. Go back to your own point of view, once again having access to all your own wisdom and experience, along with all your own values and beliefs.

Using* Their *Perceptions. Having all the knowledge and insights you gathered from experiencing the event while pretending to be in the other person's point of view, take a moment to think about what you learned:

- What did it feel like? What did you physically sense?
- What was it like using their tone of voice with the same inflections? Did it change the meaning of the message in any way?
- What do you think their facial expressions and hand gestures were trying to say?
- Doing all these things, what could they possibly be thinking or believing that would make them think that what they are saying and doing is the best way to interact with you?
- What are they focusing on as they communicate with you?
- Think about what would have needed to happen in your life that would lead you to believe that using their words and actions is the right choice? Have you ever personally communicated with someone in the same manner they did with you (without intending to be hurtful)?
- Think about how you imagined them experiencing your communication, and ask yourself if you are truly sending the message you intended to send? Are your facial expressions, posture, tone of voice and gestures congruent with your words, or is there something you could do differently that might be more effective?

Now, I can hear some of you already saying, "But this is all just childish 'make believe' and 'pretend'. How is this going to help me deal with a real bully?"

> ***Bullies aren't truly malicious; they are merely too self-focused to care whether or not their behavior negatively affects other people.***

Well... yes, I do realize this is all just imagined... and so are our thoughts and beliefs that a person is actually trying to hurt our feelings or insult us - those are just thoughts in our mind, too. The key to not being limited by your beliefs is to remember that you do not always have to believe what you think.

Insinuations and implied statements which you perceive to be the unspoken meaning of another person's words or actions are only conceived in your mind. The fact is, rarely does anyone actually follow up with a bully to verify those hidden meanings which they perceive to be the true underlying message of that person's words and behaviors.

A useful awareness to try and maintain when using verbal self defense is that bullies aren't truly malicious - bullies are simply too self-focused and don't actually care whether or not their behavior negatively affects someone else. Even in situations where a bully directly attacks someone, internally their mind is focused on their own needs for power and self-esteem. It's merely the by-product of this selfish attitude that is often harmful to the mental and emotional well-being of the person being bullied.

So, if you're going to instinctually mind-read what the other person 'really' means by their words or actions, why would you choose to think they mean something that will leave you feeling hurt or sad? It's better to choose to think they just don't realize how abusive their communication is. When you open yourself up to that way of thinking, then you can effectively use the information you get by imagining the interaction from the other person's point of view (without any of your own preconceptions or expectations).

DEVELOPING YOUR SKILLS & ABILITIES…

UNDERSTANDING BULLYING BEHAVIOR

CHOOSE A BULLYING BEHAVIOR. Look back at the list we covered in Part I about *Recognizing Bullying Behavior* and consider which behaviors you personally believe to be inappropriate or unacceptable. Take a sheet of paper and write down one of those examples of bullying behavior which you've been the victim of.

TAKE THE BULLY OUT OF THE BEHAVIOR. Now, imagine doing that behavior to someone else. Pretend you were the person treating someone that way and, at this point, remember that everything a person does has a higher positive intention. So, abusive behavior is not consciously intended to be hurtful (although that may seem difficult to believe) - the truth is that no one honestly gets up in the morning thinking, "When I go into the office I'm so going to make that guy feel horrible!" That is, unless they believe you were bullying them first… in which case they're not trying to be a bully; they're seem themselves as a vigilante who's seeking revenge.

In this case, as you imagine doing the bullying behavior yourself, think about what possible reasons or situations in which you might treat someone this way, even if it's merely accidental or unintentional. Then write down how it could be possible that you could create the perception that this behavior is justified - is it to have control, get something, feel good, etc.

To help, ask yourself the following questions: Has there ever been a time in your life you've treated someone this way without intentionally meaning to hurt them? What might you need to think about how they have treated you in order to feel you're right in acting this way? In what kind of family environment would you have grown up learning that this is the proper way to behave toward others? What series of events would need to happen in your day to create the situation where you'd act like this?

GIVE YOURSELF MORE CHOICE. So, if you chose to believe that a person who is treating you this way was *not* acting with malice intent, how much less hurtful would it feel? Rather than taking it as an attack, give the person the benefit of the doubt and pretend that they really thought that what they were saying or doing was the best reaction available to them.

Imagine that they never thought you would consider it as bullying and think about how that would assist you in being able to handle the situation differently. Now write down a few choices you could at least consider doing instead of getting defensive.

To get really good at controlling the way you connect to how others treat you, start by doing this exercise using a bullying behavior which is mildly annoying. Then try it again with progressively more abusive and inappropriate behaviors. Each time, focus on letting go of your perceived hurtful intention and choose to think that the person does not realize how mean their words or actions are.

Taking on a more understanding point of view think of more useful ways you can address their behavior instead of just putting up with it or worse, putting them in their place.

In situations where you do believe the person does mean something which is not specifically expressed, or times when you do think the bully is just trying to be mean, remember that you can always check. Believe it or not, you are free to actually ask the person if what you perceive as an underlying meaning of their communication is accurate. As an example you can ask if they really meant their tone of voice to be condescending or not. Similarly, you can ask the person to clarify the meaning of any of their communication - facial expressions, tone of voice, gestures, and even particular words or phrases.

By comparison it's just as valuable to consider whether or not you are sending the message you mean to send. After experiencing the event from their point of view, ask yourself if you are using the best tone, gestures, facial expression, body language and choice of words that support the meaning you want to give to your communication. Did the message you received when being in their position equate to what you are really trying to tell them?

FUNDAMENTAL LESSONS & LEARNINGS...

- The odds of two people having the same perception of a single event are astronomical and, in the same way, two people having the same meaning for a single word is just as unlikely.
- Other people in this world are behaving and communicating based upon their own inner mental map of the world, not yours.
- Our goal is to utilize the other person's mental map of the world in order to get them to understand the message we are trying to send them.
- No matter what a person is saying or doing, the basic premise always remains that, "Based on all their past knowledge combined with their perception of the current situation, their present behavior is the best choice available to them in order to get their needs met". If the person was aware of a better option which would effectively deal with the situation and still achieve their higher intention, then their unconscious mind would choose that one instead.
- Bullies are not consciously malicious - they are simply too self-focused to care whether or not their words and actions hurt other people.
- When you are taking on another person's point of view the most important thing to remember is to suspend your own values and beliefs before you imagine what they are experiencing. This allows you to experience the event (including your own communication towards them) without any pre-existing expectations or judgments.

ALL THE ON-LOOKERS THINK...

"Ask two witnesses from either side of the street about the same accident and you'll begin to question the history books."
Jodie Gastel

Have you ever noticed that people always seem to stop and stare whenever something interesting happens? It's like human curiosity drives us to take a never ending interest in life going on around us. We all want to know what's happening and we try to understand it in order to determine if it has any consequences or implications towards us personally. The possibility of an incident spilling over and becoming our problem is a concern that everyone thinks about at some level.

In NLP, being an outsider simply watching an experience from the sidelines is commonly referred to as taking an observer's role or the Observer Point of View. Similar to taking on another person's point of view, the observer's point of view is useful for gathering information.

The perspective of a witness who experiences the communication between two people (without taking part in the interaction) will be very different than the perception of anyone directly involved. An outsider can often see things which the people too close to the situation are not aware of.

So you might think that these three points of view - your own, the other person's and an observer's - are the only points of view which exist; however, there is one other perspective useful to verbal self defense in the workplace. That point of view is the Organization's Point of View.

Are you wondering, "How can an organization or company have its own perspective?" It's essentially the concept of a group mind, team spirit, or the office environment - all of these are comparative to what an organization's perspective is. They include things like organizational policies and procedures as well as cultural and community beliefs and values.

If you think about it, in some cultures of the world it is customary to bow when greeting someone, while in other cultures two people might simply shake hands. In some businesses people are expected to address supervisors and bosses formally while in other companies it's common to call them by their first name. In every organization there are expected ways of interacting, some of which are written rules which cannot be broken (or are not supposed to be broken) and others are unspoken expectations which might be more flexible. All of these components are combined to make up the group's perceptions, also called the Organization's Point of View.

When you identify the organization's collective characteristics it allows you to work more effectively within its structure and guidelines. One core value which most businesses have is the requirement of professionalism. In order to provide customer care using this type of a disposition a staff member needs to take into account the organization's point of view in order to ensure all rules and regulations are being met. At the same time this person is also expected by society to still adhere to cultural and personal expectations as well.

What this means is that a person who is acting professionally is always working to find balance between the needs of the organization, cultural expectations and their own personal beliefs and values. On its own this can often be difficult. Now, add on top of all that an interaction involving an aggressive and abusive communicator who feels they are not limited by any of those things. At that point the dynamics of the situation become almost unfathomable, and yet, it happens every day in businesses around the globe.

The trick to making it work is to consider the organization's point of view by itself, without applying any of your own judgments. Considering the way you communicate from the organization's point of view allows you to recognize the limitations on how you are able to use verbal self defense.

As a bonus, recognizing the organization's perceptions gives you the ability to reduce your own emotional reactions to situations which you do not need to take so personally. Like when a client attacks the reputation of your company. In that case, by using the organization's point of view it's possible to separate yourself from the comments and avoid taking it as an attack against you personally.

The Observer's Point of View

The best way of explaining the observer position is to consider it like the point of view of a curious, little alien scientist from outer-space who has come to Earth to study human interpersonal communication. In order to get a good observer point of view on a situation simply ask yourself, "If an alien scientist were here documenting the interaction between all the people involved without trying to interpret them or judge them, what would he write down?"

The type of things he might put in his report will only include stuff that could be documented on film, such as the words that were spoken, tones of voice people used, gestures they made, facial expressions they made, the posturing they took and even the way they physically touched each other. The one limitation the little alien has is that he cannot read people's minds so he does not know what the people are thinking or feeling as they are communicating with one another.

Using the observer's point of view you start by imagining being outside yourself in a point of view completely detached from anyone involved. Watch and listen to the event like a fly on the wall - an interested, but neutral, observer. It can be helpful if you are in a symmetrical and relaxed posture when you are imagining being in the observer position. Also, try to refer to all the people involved using third person language such as she, he and they (this includes the actual 'You' in the experience along with everyone else in their own points of view).

Using the observer's point of view effectively requires you to once again suspend any and all beliefs, values and assumptions that might exist in your own point of view. This is so the information you gather from watching and listening to the interaction as it happens is only that - just information, without any meaning or judgment. By suppressing all the beliefs, values and understandings that a person may use to filter their perceptions of the interaction you can witness the event without experiencing any feelings. When you are free from emotional responses then you can get curious about what the intentions are behind the people's communication and whether or not it is actually working to express those intended messages.

Any little, green alien who has no prior knowledge of the people or situation would be limited to only using what he sees and hears in order to understand the event. When you have gathered all that information from the observer position you can take it back to your own point of view in order to consider it. Think about what forms of communication were actually useful in getting their message across. As well, take note of what you could do differently to be more effective (this applies to both sending and receiving messages). It's also beneficial to question whether or not the interaction is actually accomplishing anything - is there clear understanding and useful communication between the people involved or is the conversation just going nowhere?

DEVELOPING YOUR SKILLS & ABILITIES…

GOING OUTSIDE TO SEE IN

Each day we go through life interacting with all the people around us talking, listening, trying to understand others while, at the same time, trying to get others to understand us. The difficulty begins when we start to feel that people are either unable or unwilling to make sense of our communication, so we end up not feeling listened to or cared about.

When that happens it will eventually cause aggravation, frustration, annoyance or any number of other bad feelings. At that point our communication tactics turn ugly and the interaction begins to shift from a polite conversation towards a heated argument. This process, although easy to spot for an onlooker, will often go unnoticed by the participants themselves until it has turned confrontational.

WATCH IT ALL HAPPEN. The simple truth is that disagreements happen all the time in our world and you will find them in the home, in the office and even out in the general public. A good way to practice observation skills is to watch an argument from the outside in order to see what went wrong.

Choose any movie from the drama section of your local video store, then go home and watch it. The first scene you come to where two people are having any type of intense discussion stop the movie and back it up to the beginning of the scene.

Now, watch the entire scene from start to finish and then write a very short explanation of what the discussion seemed to be about. Avoid writing a summarization of what you think the topic was and instead write down specific phrases from the actual scene that the people used to define or identify what the disagreement was about.

LISTEN TO THE WORDS. If necessary you can watch the scene again and then write down words and phrases that each person used to describe their own point of view in this conflict. Take note of whether or not you think the words they used effectively represented what they actually meant, or is it possible there was an unspoken or implied message that went with their tone of voice or body language.

Notice the Unspoken Messages. It's a fact that the majority of human communication happens non-verbally, so at this point go through the scene again and listen and watch for any non-verbal cues. Notice what the people used in order to add emphasis or a deeper meaning to their communication.

Avoid defining what the deeper meaning was or why they emphasized something, just make note of body language, facial expressions, tone of voice, etc. that either person used. As an example, rather than saying someone emphasized how dumb the other person's comment was, specifically describe what they did to send that message, such as, "He/she said 'Duh' in a low and drawn out tone of voice."

Recognize the Useful Communication. Watching it again consider: What seemed to work in getting the conflict resolved (if it was resolved)? Write down parts of the interaction such as words, actions, tone of voice, facial expression, posture, etc. which created the greatest amount of understanding and clarity between the people involved. Again, instead of saying things like, "He gave her a look of 'understanding'," use specific descriptions such as, "He looked directly at her with raised eyebrows and a slight smile."

Change Communication That Isn't Working. By now you've probably watched the scene a few times so, during the progress of the argument, did you notice anything that just did not seem to work, or perhaps even made things worse? Describe anything that either person did or said which led to further misunderstandings or escalated the disagreement.

Effective Communication in Your Life. Having watched the process for creating this disagreement in the movie, now think about your own life. List out behaviors, tone of voice, facial expressions, body posture, gestures, phrases, or specific words you personally would consider good communication skills.

What are things you think people should say or do whenever possible in order to avoid risking an argument in the real world? What kinds of tones of voice help create useful, open communication between people? Are there any particular questions or phrases which you think help create more effective communicate between people? What else can you do that will help create more open and useful interactions with others?

Take time to review that final list you made in the last exercise - the one outlining things you described as Good Communication Skills. Put a checkmark next to all the ones you consistently remember to do when interacting with other people… not the ones you believe you already do, only the ones which you actually think of during a discussion and consciously choose to do.

Take a bright colored highlighter and highlight all the others - these are the ones which you want to work on *remembering* during your daily interactions with people. Practice thinking of these skills in your everyday conversations so you get good at remembering them. This allows them to be integrated in your unconscious mind as healthy habits so they will naturally come to mind when you're dealing with a bully.

For some people there might be quite a few things highlighted so, at first, choose just one thing you want to learn and then focus on remembering it in 3 conversations each day for a week. In the beginning you may only remember after you finish talking with someone, but as the week progresses you will remember to do it sooner and sooner until finally you are thinking of it during your interaction with a person.

Whether or not you remember to do it during every conversation is irrelevant because some skills may not apply to certain interactions. It's simply the act of *remembering to think about doing it during a conversation* that is important. That way the choice will be available to you when it's needed and you will think to do it in the times when it can actually make a difference.

THE ORGANIZATION'S POINT OF VIEW

You already know that every person has their own individual values and beliefs about life, but what if that person's internal perceptions of the world overlap with other people's perceptions? What do you think happens then? Well, that's a good question and I'm glad you're thinking about that!

> ***Any actions or behaviors outside the cultural rules of the group mind will be considered inappropriate or unprofessional.***

It's true that, against the odds, people's mental maps will occasionally overlap and be so similar that they seem to be the same. This is going to happen whenever a group of people come together on a regular basis. The members of the group develop a deeper level of interpersonal rapport with each other and, as they do, they begin to discover ways to relate to one another on that deeper level of personal values and beliefs.

As this begins to happen, people in the general group will start to discover ways of thinking and doing things which the majority of the group agrees to be right or wrong. This perceived level of congruency creates an unspoken type of understanding between group members - a kind of *unconsciously agreed upon set of limits and expectations* which everyone must follow in order to be considered part of the group.

Any actions or behaviors outside these Cultural Rules will be considered by the group as inappropriate and unacceptable. For this reason a good verbal defender needs to recognize this group mentality and take it into account when deciding on a course of action.

In many cases organizations and businesses will often have some of these expected guidelines even written down. They are commonly referred to as the company's Policies and Procedures. Mainly they are put in place as a way to ensure everyone has an equal understanding of what will and will not be acceptable in the office environment.

One familiar example would be a well written Sexual Harassment Policy which would include clear descriptions of specific behaviors that are unacceptable such as, "...conversations or inquiries of a sexual nature or which use any labels generally considered descriptive of sexual parts of the human anatomy are strictly prohibited". On the other hand, poorly written Sexual Harassment Policies exist and will usually have generalized terms and explanations like, "...it is best to refrain from using unprofessional language in the office," - a description which is almost entirely left up to individual interpretation. Policies like these are ineffective because, as we know, everyone will have their own unique interpretation based on their personal mental map.

Going beyond the organization's formal policies, procedures, rules and regulations there also exists the general office atmosphere where particular attitudes, behaviors and interactions are simply implied or presumed. There is usually an adjustment period when a person first starts working at a new job in which they learn these generally accepted and understood guidelines of how the people in this specific workplace interact.

Office bullying is usually disguised as part of these unwritten behaviors which appear to be just part of the way the office is run. Since the words and actions of the bully are not directly addressed in the company's written rules and regulations it means that a verbal defender might need to defend themselves from both the bully and the group mind as well. Whenever abusive words and actions are considered normal it means that the group majority considers them acceptable and the bully consequently feels their behavior is condoned by the organization. The end result is; to overcome office bullying, verbal self defense may need to be applied against both the workplace bully and the person responsible for general working conditions (such as a Personnel Manager).

Whether you're confronting the organizational culture, a group mindset, or simply working within the generally expected guidelines of the office atmosphere, it's valuable for a good verbal defender to accept that these rules (written and unwritten) exist and they should identify and clarify them before committing to any particular plan of action. To do this the process is different than taking on another person's point of view - in order to properly understand an organization's point of view it requires more fore-thought and consideration.

DEVELOPING YOUR SKILLS & ABILITIES...

GETTING INTO THE GROUP MINDSET

The *Group Mentality* of an organization includes both the perceptions of the people involved as well as the mission and purpose of the business itself. Combining these two things together will give you a sense of the overall mindset in that environment, and these will be your basic guiding limits when determining your own course of action.

Why you use verbal self defense will be based upon your own values and beliefs while, in order to be as effective as possible, *how* you use it will be based upon the organization's accepted beliefs, behaviors, attitudes and interactions. So, take a piece of paper and write out the following:

WHAT THE BUSINESS WANTS. Start by asking yourself, "What is the focus of the business?" Specifically, write down what people do in the business in order for it to make money. This can include its services, products, or even the Corporate Mission Statement. Be certain to underline anything that specifically defines any part of the expected working environment for the organization's staff and employees.

THE WRITTEN RULES. Next, it's necessary to know what expectations are already set down in writing. So, get a copy of the company policies, procedures, rules and regulations and then read through them and make note of any specific behaviors that are identified as unacceptable. Be sure to also notice how descriptive their explanations are for any such behaviors.

If possible, list all these out in two columns - one column for what staff members are expected to do and one column for what they are expected *not* to do. Now put a star beside each one that has clearly defined consequences/rewards, and circle the ones that are unclear, unknown by staff or simply not enforced.

THE UNWRITTEN RULES. Take a moment and think about what the interactions among employees are usually like around your workplace. Consider what it's commonly like to deal with your supervisors, staff, co-workers, customers and clients.

Now, list out both the acceptable and unacceptable behaviors that you notice happening in the office on a day-to-day basis. How do people usually treat one another? How do they commonly talk to each other?

Underline anything which directly violates the written rules from above and then circle all the ones that you feel are mentally and/or emotionally hurtful to people.

After all that, look to see if any interactions counteract one another. For example, are there any positive behaviors used to make negative ones more acceptable? Things like giving promotions to people who are willing to tolerate the boss's abuse.

Where It All Comes From. Remember that all the written and unwritten rules and expectations come out of the group's common values and beliefs. So now you want to identify what particular beliefs about the world must the majority of people in your workplace need to have in order for them to act the way they do.

What does the way everyone treats each other say about the beliefs and values they have in their mental maps? What kind of personal values would support these behaviors? What is the intention of, or purpose for, doing those things or talking that way?

An example might be if people often stay to work a little late in order to finish up a job or if people take time to do a few extra steps in order to make the job look better; those kinds of behaviors might lead you to think that, "People in the office value doing a good job and believe it's important to do good work". The key is to describe what values and beliefs you think causes them to do the behaviors you've seen.

As well, consider if a behavior provides any benefit to the overall working environment, for the business as a whole, or for any certain individuals? One example is, in some companies, profanity is considered acceptable because it seems to create a more relaxed working environment.

> *WHAT YOU AGREE WITH.* Having written out a bunch of personal beliefs and values about the world which you think people in your workplace use to justify their behaviors (both good and bad), you should go through the list and mark off which beliefs/values you can agree with and which ones you cannot.

I realize that people don't usually think of their job this way so take a few minutes to review everything you have written about how people interact in your workplace and what the underlying expectations, beliefs and values are that support such behaviors. What, in all this, do you agree with and what do you feel is inappropriate, unacceptable or intolerable? Have you had to put up with any of these things in the last week or the last month? And after all that, are there any parts of this that need to be addressed in order to stop bullying in your workplace?

Now, also look for any generally accepted policies, procedures, expectations or beliefs generally considered to be part of the office environment (written or unwritten) which could help you in standing up to a bully? It's useful to make note of any cultural beliefs and values or behavioral expectations that you can bring up while using your verbal self defense which the group mind will support - anything that you can use to convince the bully to stop their inappropriate behavior.

After you've gone through this process and determined what the organization's point of view is with regard to its goals, its preferred way of handling things and the group mindset, then it's time to recognize these are the rules, guidelines and boundaries that your verbal self defense tactics must work within.

Much like physical self defense has spatial limitations such as ground & terrain, buildings & walls, furniture & objects, verbal self defense in the workplace has company policies and office politics that may set expectations of how to appropriately address the bully, or there may be procedures that can influence whether or not your verbal self defense tactics will be successful.

If, in the case of physical bullying, you tried to run away but didn't see there was a table in your way, and consequently you started to run before you noticed the obstacle, it's possible that running into the table might cause you more injury than the bully would have. In the same way, if you try to verbally defend yourself and attempt to use a form of communication, such as a particular tone of voice that is considered inappropriate in the office, you could end up getting in more trouble than the bully.

FUNDAMENTAL LESSONS & LEARNINGS...

- The *Observer's Point of View* is when you perceive an experience as if watching from the sidelines, limited to only what you can see and hear - information gathered from this position is useful in deciding what communication is working, what is not and what could be done differently in order to be more effective.
- To use the observer's point of view effectively it's necessary to suspend any and all beliefs, values and assumptions that might normally filter your perceptions - any information gathered from the observer's position should be taken without any underlying meaning or implication.
- An *Organization's Point of View* is essentially the concept of a group mindset or office environment. This includes company policies and procedures as well as cultural and community beliefs and values.
- To be a more effective verbal defender it's important to use an organization's point of view like a set of guidelines to help you decide how you will apply any tactics of verbal self defense.

PART III

KNOW YOUR SELF

You know how to walk, how to talk, how to dress yourself and feed yourself. It's certain you know how to read if you're reading this book. Whatever it is you know, we can say you are certain that you know what it is you know, but you did not *always* know what you now know - you had to learn it!

It might seem a bit simple to say it, but human beings learn things through their experiences. This means that whenever you have an experience, your brain attempts to derive the most valuable lesson or learning from that event. The interesting thing to realize now is that we learn to feel bad about being bullied in the same way we learn everything else.

IMAGINE...

In every culture, as children grow up they are expected to learn how to identify things such as objects, people, and concepts like time, space, etc. Often this is accomplished with the help and guidance of parents and teachers. One specific experience children learn growing up is how to put a name, or label, to their feelings as they are taught what emotions are.

LEARNING AN EMOTION. After having a bad experience on the playground a young child runs to their mommy or daddy crying. When the parent asks, "What's the matter?" the child's reply is, "I didn't like it!"

The parent, in an effort to understand, asks, "Were you scared?"

With a look of confusion the child responds quizzically, "I don't know. I just didn't like it."

Believing they have identified what has happened the parent simply states, "Oh. You were scared." Now the child has been given the label of *scared* to describe what they're feeling.

CONFIRMING THE LEARNING. The next time the child experiences something unpleasant on the playground they come running to the parent once again crying, "I didn't like that!"

This time, when the parent asks, "Were you scared?" the child can then remember the last time they heard the term *scared* and compare what they feel now to what they felt during that event.

Thinking that they are similar feelings, the child might respond by saying, "Yeah... (*sniffle*) ... I was scared." Without hesitation the parent responds by comforting the child and so the child gets an immediate sense of being understood.

THE LEARNED EMOTION. At some point in the future, the child once again comes running to the parent crying, "That scared me!" Immediately the parent understands and begins to comfort the young child, thus reinforcing the sense of being understood and confirming once again that the child's connection of the label *scared* to what they are feeling is correct.

This is the point where the lesson goes from mere coincidence to a recognized pattern and is taken on as knowledge which allows the child to believe they know what *scared* means. The problem is that from this point forward the child believes that everyone experiences fear the same way as they do - that everyone has the same physical sensations in their body that tell them when they are scared.

This process works for learning all the different types of emotions. Someone at some time in our past helped us to identify emotional labels like fear, sadness, guilt, joy, love, curiosity, etc., and we connected them to the feelings we experienced during the event.

As we get older, it becomes more and more natural to simply feel an emotion, recognize it with a label and then move forward. Eventually we begin to forget the labels completely and simply experience the emotions of life, only defining what exactly we're feeling when it's necessary to explain it to others. Even in those rare cases we simply put a label to it without any further clarification.

Since it is common for people to avoid talking about their emotions at work, it even gets to a point where we stop connecting to the feelings altogether. We then just focus on and jump to the explanation of why we feel what we do, even if we're not actually certain we know what it is we're feeling. A common example of this is when someone automatically begins to explain themselves without being asked to. It was a feeling that caused them to believe they must justify their decision, however, they're not consciously aware of having experienced the feeling in that moment - they merely react to it.

As we get older, it becomes more and more natural to simply feel an emotion, recognize it with a label and then move on.

In verbal self defense you want to reconnect with how you identify your emotions. When you become more attuned to the original sensations beneath your feelings, you can then pinpoint the actual cause of mental and emotional abuse. This allows you to have an ability to pick out the specific words and actions of others which cause you to feel bullied, and those are the things that verbal self defense is designed to deal with directly.

FUNDAMENTAL LESSONS & LEARNINGS...

- You learn emotions the same way you learn everything else - through experiencing them and being taught to label those experiences.
- Having the ability to reconnect with the source which causes you to feel bullied will give you the awareness you need in order to stop someone from bullying you.

Are You Upset About Something?

"I'm struck by the insidious, computer-driven tendency to take things out of the domain of muscular activity and put them into the domain of mental activity. The transfer is not paying off. Sure, muscles are unreliable, but they represent several million years of accumulated finesse."
Brian Eno

"How do you feel today?" It seems like a straight forward question, but have you noticed that no one ever answers that question? Everyone assumes that what a person means by the question is, "What emotion are you feeling the most today?" That's the easier of the two questions to answer because most people know what kind of mood they are in. The original question is much more difficult to answer because it requires a greater degree of self-awareness.

No one ever seems very interested in knowing *how* they feel the emotion they are experiencing; however, there is much more value for you as a verbal defender to recognize *how* you sense an emotion rather than *what* emotion you are feeling. Trust me, you probably know when you are upset or angry or sad or whatever other emotion. The key instead is to sense it coming before it happens. When you can sense your emotions shifting or building then you can verbally defend yourself before you feel bullied or hurt.

Strategists throughout history have agreed that there are times when the best defense is a good offense. The difficulty is that you must make your move at just the right time. All great martial artists know that timing plays a huge role in applying their skills effectively, and the same thing goes for verbal self defense. If you act too early then you become the bully, and if you act too late then you are fighting to overcome the feeling of being bullied.

IT'S CALLED KINESTHESIA

We all experience feelings every day whether we are aware of them or not. Sometimes you will feel happy, sad, annoyed, tired, bored, excited, motivated, etc. The question to ask yourself is, "How do you know when you are feeling something?"

It seems simple enough to figure out; however, it suddenly becomes more complex when we actually try to explain it. We might be aware when we are feeling frustrated by something, like when someone is talking to us in a condescending tone of voice. We know when we feel frustrated, but the real question is, "How do we know we are frustrated?" or "What tells you that you're frustrated?"

The most common answer people give is, "Because I am!" with no clear recognition of what's happening inside their own body and mind that tells them how they recognize the feeling of frustration. In the same way we don't know how we are able to tell the difference between being frustrated and being angry, or the difference between mildly annoyed and severely pissed-off; however, you do recognize that there is a difference. As we were growing up we got so used to just identifying our feelings we lost touch with the actual internal information that told us how we know what we're feeling.

Even worse, as your mind learned to get better and better at filtering out that information from within yourself that tells you what emotion you are experiencing, you also lost connection with the feelings that preceded it - the sensations you feel as the emotion first starts to grow and get stronger. Some people become so separated from their emotions that they can end up being surprised when a really powerful emotion comes on. For people like this, before they even realize how upset they are, the moment to do something either passes them by or they do something without conscious control. Anyone who has ever said something hurtful during an argument and, as it was coming out of their mouth, wished they could have taken it back has experienced this. That's because you just said it without thinking and your reaction was as much a surprise to you as it was to the listener.

You need to have a connection to how you know a feeling is coming so you can be prepared to do something before the emotion takes control and causes your unconscious mind to make you do something without your permission.

For further clarification…

Awareness of Muscle Sensations

Kinesthesia is the scientific term which refers to the ability of the body's sensory organs within our muscles, tendons and joints to notice and respond to stimulation. This is sometimes called *Tactile Awareness.*

For that reason, most references to kinesthetic awareness are about your sensations when you are touching something. However, beyond that original moment of contact with the object, within the mind, there remains an imprint of that tactile awareness, allowing you to remember what the sensations felt like at any time in the future.

In the same way, whenever the muscles and organs in your body send a message to the brain there is a form of *kinesthetic awareness.* As an example, someone jumps out and surprises you and your instinctual freeze, flight, fight and fright response causes the brain to trigger a release of adrenaline into the body so you are ready to react in whatever way is necessary. Your muscles' responses to that extra burst of adrenaline are sent to the brain as a type of kinesthetic sensation in order to confirm to the brain they have received the adrenaline and they're ready to go.

Those kinesthetic sensations are what you're aware of when you identify the experience as frightening or shocking. In the mind those sensations are combined with your visual and auditory input to create a memory of the event.

As verbal defenders, the main thing to focus on at this point is the set of original kinesthetic sensations which identified the *feeling* of being bullied. We want to separate those feelings from the other auditory and visual components of the experience because it's those sensations alone that your mind uses to identifying the emotions that you experience when being bullied, regardless of who, where, when or why it's happening.

As another way of thinking about it, kinesthetic sensations relate to any bodily sensation; including both tactile (external touch) and visceral (sensations inside the body). Later in the book, it's going to be your own visceral sensations which you will use to determine the best possible timing and automatically trigger your verbal defense tactics.

So, all emotions are actually just feelings of sensations in our body (thus we come to call them feelings). One main characteristic which emotions have that differs from the endless number of other sensations we experience in our body during a day is that emotions are not one single kinesthetic sensation by themselves. Rather, each emotion can be defined by a specific set of sensations that happen all together (either all at one time, or in a certain order, or possibly some combination thereof).

For further clarification…

A Sensational Experiment

Most people in our world have some level of stress in their life, and workplace bullying does a good deal to increase it. Stress is an emotional state just like any other, which means that everyone has a specific set of unique kinesthetic sensations to identify it.

Think about how you notice when you feel stressed and what you actually feel in your body when you're stressed. Everyone will experience stress differently, so the best is to start by recalling a situation in your past when you really experienced a sense of intense stress. Remember a one-time event in your past where you felt highly stressed, and then start by rewinding the memory of the event back to a few minutes before any sensations of stress ever began.

Now, the trick is to be certain you're experiencing the memory from inside your own awareness. Sometimes people remember situations or experiences and, rather than imagining the event by seeing things through their own eyes, people put themselves in the picture like they're watching themselves in a movie. This way of thinking is useful if you want to avoid feeling the emotions in a memory but that's the opposite of what we want to do in this case.

For now, choose the memory and remember how it happened as seen through your eyes, feeling the feelings in your own body, hearing what you heard with your own ears. As you go through the process, try to focus your awareness on what kinesthetic sensations you noticed in your body as you progress forward through events in your memory.

How did you know you were feeling stress? Was there tension in your body? What kind of sensations did you experience? Where in your body did you feel things? Ask yourself questions like those in order to really become aware of all the sensations you experienced in that stressful event.

Some people may feel tension in their shoulders, or clenching of their fists, a sensation of weight on their chest, perhaps a tingling in their stomach, or any number of other possibilities. It could be one sensation at a time or several sensations all at once. What was the experience of stress like for you?

Whatever way you personally answer these questions will be unique to you. As well, things like time, place, situation, people present, etc. all affect how you experience stress in general. Thus, there may be differences between memories involving the same emotion; the base components however will remain similar in some way.

You can do all this for positive emotions too. Let go of that previous memory and try this process with a real strong feeling of happiness, or excitement, or love. As well, try the same experiment with other memories of the same emotion and see how they are similar and how they are different. Look for how you personally tell the difference between different emotions - an example would be, "What's the difference between feeling content and when you are having lots of fun?"

SENSORY AWARENESS

To have a better sense of your emotions as a verbal defender you must develop your ability to be aware of the sensations that tell you when you are experiencing an emotion, as well as what emotion it is. In the field of NLP this skill is actually called Sensory Awareness and it's the component that will eventually become the trigger for your verbal self defense skills later in this book.

You might describe this concept of *sensory awareness* best as: "A highly acute ability to notice the tiny details of the sensory input which is usually outside your awareness." This applies to both internal sensory input and external sensory input. That means good sensory awareness skills allow you to be aware of both your own internal sensations as well as things coming in through your sight, hearing, touch, taste and smell. It's interesting to note that, based on that description, sensory awareness applies to both input from inside yourself and from the person you are defending yourself against.

At this point, however, we only want to focus on recognizing the things going on in your own mind and body. For now, this deeper self-awareness will make you much more effective in your ability to communicate with others by learning to recognize when someone is bullying you. As well, it will provide you with a better sense of the right timing in order to know exactly when to take action.

Later in this book we will discuss increased sensory awareness of a bully's communication in order to more specifically identify the exact behavior(s) they are doing which upset you. This will help you beat an office bully by being clear about what specific words and actions are the bullying tactics that they need to stop.

Increasing Your Sensory Awareness

At the foundation of really good sensory awareness lies the natural ability of our human nervous system to notice differences. This natural instinct is scientifically referred to as your *Difference Threshold*. It's constantly watching for any changes, internal or external, that enter your awareness. Specifically, your mind focuses on trying to maintain a balanced and consistent sense of contentment. Whenever it notices something that signifies a diversion from that sense of contentedness - something different - then your unconscious mind starts looking for a way to return things back to balance.

An example of your difference threshold in action would be when your stomach creates the sensation of hunger. When you are not hungry you do not feel anything in your stomach. Whenever your stomach starts generating sensations which your brain identifies as hunger, you automatically start thinking about food in order to satiate those inner feelings of hunger. After you eat, the hunger sensation goes away and your tummy returns to a state of contentment (having no sensations at all). In this same way, when you feel threatened by a bully, your sense of fear triggers your instincts to freeze, flight, fight or fright.

The concern is that, by having grown up and learned all the labels, we forget about our actual feelings. As an adult it becomes more important to focus on how you are going to deal with your feelings rather than identifying them. That becomes an issue because when we stop paying attention to the deeper internal sensations which trigger our reactions we consequently lose control over how and when we choose to react - we hold, run, fight or panic without knowing why.

DEVELOPING YOUR SKILLS & ABILITIES...

NOTICING KINESTHETIC AWARENESS

Bullies don't usually have a tendency to listen very well, so a good verbal defender often needs to explain behaviors and concepts in the simplest way possible. In order to practice this you can start thinking more about how you would personally describe things you experience. If the person you were explaining it to has never experienced anything like it, how would you figure out what words you'd choose which they could most likely relate to?

Below are several experiences which all have a component of kinesthetic sensation. Take a moment and consider how someone might describe each item or event and then list some things you could say in order to explain what the physical sensation is like for you.

Describe where you feel the sensation(s); how large/small it is; if the sensation have a certain shape; what kind of intensity there is; whether or not the sensation is steady or changes; if there's a sense of movement that happens with it and, if so, what direction(s) it moves; how long the sensation(s) last; if there are any vibrations; any pressure or weight; what kind of temperature it is; etc. Attempt to describe these things in the most basic way possible so that even a person with only a rudimentary understanding of your language could figure out what you were talking about.

THIS BOOK. Hold a book in your hand. What does it feel like? How would you personally describe it? Consider things like weight, texture, size, shape, etc.

MOVE YOUR ARM. Hold your arm straight out in front of you and then move it around in a circle for 10 seconds.

What do you notice about the sensations of your arm in motion? How would you describe it?

LIE DOWN AND REST. Lay down somewhere and relax every muscle in your body. What do you feel differently than when you're walking around during your day? Find a way to describe what you personally perceive to be the difference in sensations between this state of rest and the action of walking.

IN A BATH. Remember a time you were in the bath or a hot tub. Describe your experiences. What sensations do you have in your body? How specific can you get?

IN THE SHOWER. Remember the last time you had a shower. What sensations do you feel in your body that makes it so different than being in a bath or hot tub?

EXERCISING. Think about exercising. As you imagine exercising and really pushing yourself, what sensations are you most aware of? How can you tell when you're reaching your limit?

THE HEAT IN SUMMER. Imagine a really hot day in summer. What sensations tell you this day is so much hotter than a regular summer day?

THE COLD OF WINTER. Winter has cooler days than summer and some are colder than others. Remember a really cold day that made you appreciate the summer season and explain the sensations which made it so much different than the warmer weather of summer.

Now, go back and quickly skim through what you wrote in response to this last exercise. I'm curious to know, how much of what you explained were specifically sensations you experienced in your body? How many of your descriptions included visual things you would need to see in order to understand? If you described only the physical sensations which you wrote down to someone else, do you think they could guess what you were talking about?

Take a moment and remember that everyone experiences things differently, including the sensations which identify certain objects and events in life. The important thing to keep in mind is that there will always be a basic amount of similarity in people's experiences of the same object or event. It's these base similarities in people's experience of something which we are trying to get a person to connect with when we are explaining it to them - the previous exercise is designed to help bring those foundational similarities into your awareness so that you can be more effective when trying to explain yourself to a bully.

Even though everyone has their own unique mental map regarding objects and events in life, there will always be some base similarities.

Being Aware of Your Emotions

Back in pre-school, when our teachers were showing us how to recognize emotions they would often show a bunch of different faces, and each one would have unique mouth and eyes which were meant to show us a different facial expression. The basic idea is to help kids learn what to look for in other people's facial expressions in order to recognize what emotion someone is feeling - to teach us what base similarities there should be in expressing certain emotions like happy, or sad, or angry, etc.

In essence this is a good idea. Learning to use what we *see* in order to relate to what other people *feel*. When we did something that hurt someone else mom and dad used to ask us, "...and how do you think they felt when you did that?" Their intention was to teach us sympathy and (as we've already covered) it's the key component of the old adage, "Do unto others as you'd have done unto you". The problem arises when we start using only what we see in order to recognize other people's emotions - we stop using our own kinesthetic sensations as a reference.

When people start applying a visual way of understanding emotion to themselves it never works because they try and create a picture of themselves in their own mind and use that image to figure out what they're feeling. That can be a problem when you can't actually see yourself. To truly recognize your own emotions you need to *feel* it in your body, and to do this effectively requires a little extra effort and focus than most people normally give themselves.

DEVELOPING YOUR SKILLS & ABILITIES…

INTERNAL NOTIONS OF EMOTIONS

Since you store both positive and negative emotions in your body as kinesthetic sensations, you can use your awareness of these sensations to determine whether or not the way someone is communicating with you is appropriate and acceptable to you. To do this, however, you must be able to recognize the difference between good feelings and bad feelings.

Using two different events from your past it's possible to bring into your awareness how the sensations of positive and negative emotions are different for you.

YOUR NEGATIVE EMOTIONS. Choose a negative emotion. Pick any unpleasant emotion like anger, sadness, hurt, guilt, jealousy or fear. Decide which one you want to have more awareness about and better control over.

After you choose one, keep that emotion in mind and think back to a significant event in your past where you felt that emotion fully and completely. As you remember it now, recall what happened and what you went through. Re-experience the event in your mind, paying attention to your senses so you see what you saw, hear what you heard, feel what you felt, etc.

Now rewind the memory and go through it again focusing specifically on the kinesthetic sensations inside you. Describe the sensations that you notice in your body as you re-live the memory:

- In what part of your body do you feel the sensations?
- How large or small are the feelings you sense in your body?
- Are the sensations localized to a particular part of your body? If not, is it all over or does it move around? If it moves around, is there any pattern to the way it moves through your body?

- What is the intensity of the sensation like during the course of the experience?
- Are the sensations steady or do they change during the event? If they change, in what way do they change?
- Is there any sense of movement in your body? If so, in what direction(s)?
- Do you feel vibrations of any kind?
- Is there any amount of pressure or weight in, around or upon your body?
- Do you feel any particular temperature, and if so, does it change or remain constant?
- How long do the sensations last? Are the sensations constant or do they come and go?
- Is there anything else you notice about the sensations you experience?

YOUR POSITIVE EMOTIONS. Now, go through the same process you used for the negative emotion above, but this time choose a positive emotion. Pick an emotion which you want to experience more in your life, like happiness, joy, love, excitement, confidence, etc.

Once again, keeping that positive emotion in mind, remember an event in your past where you really felt that positive feeling totally and completely. And as you are remembering the event now, re-experience everything through your own senses, seeing what you saw, hearing what you heard, feeling what you felt, etc.

When you are ready, rewind the memory and go through it again describing only the sensations you notice in your body as you move through the memory:

- In what part of your body do you feel the sensations?
- How large or small are the feelings you sense in your body?
- Are the sensations localized to that particular part of your body? If not, is it all over? Or, if it moves around, is there any pattern to the way it moves through your body?

- What is the intensity of the sensation like during the course of the memory?
- Are the sensations steady or do they change? If they change, in what way do they change?
- Is there any sense of movement in your body? If so, describe it.
- Do you feel vibrations of any kind?
- Is there any amount of pressure or weight in, around or upon your body?
- Do you feel any particular temperature, and if so, does it change or remain constant?
- How long do the sensations last? Are the sensations constant or do they come and go?
- Is there anything else you notice about the sensations you experience?

Continue to focus on developing your own sensory awareness by being mindful of the sensations in your body when you feel any emotions. At least 3 times a day for a week try noticing what emotion you're feeling and the sensations which define that emotion for you. With practice you'll soon start to be more aware and more in control of the emotions you experience in life - you find a greater ability to choose when you want to be happy and when you want to be sad.

Having now gone through the process of getting back in touch with the sensations that you feel when you experience both a positive and a negative emotion, it's important to note that every emotion, positive or negative, will be different. No two positive emotions will be the same and no two negative emotions will be the same - that means happy and sad will each have their own set of kinesthetic sensations. Comparatively, degrees of the same emotion can have similarities - mildly annoyed and fully frustrated can have some basic similarities that will allow you to know they're related.

Considering that every conceivable emotion will have its own way of being stored kinesthetically in your body, it means that each time you want to determine what behavior is connected to a specific emotion you will need to take a moment to be aware of how you recognize that particular emotion in yourself. So, if someone pushes your buttons and you feel angry, the question is: "What is it inside yourself that tells you that you're angry?" Knowing the sensations which identify anger means you can catch it just as it starts, and use verbal self defense to stop whatever the person is doing, before you get really angry.

Luckily, each time you stop to notice the kinesthetic sensations behind an emotion, the process will become easier and more natural. Eventually, with time and practice, you will be able to recognize your own emotions at any moment in time, in any situation. As your self-awareness of emotions increases, so will your ability to control what you choose to feel and how intense you will allow that feeling to be. Instead of your emotions controlling you, you will be able to control your emotions.

From a purely verbal self defense angle we want to focus on noticing how our mind and body generate the feelings of being bullied so that we can use that greater awareness as a means to direct our actions when dealing with bullies. Along with noticing the kinesthetic sensations underneath your feeling of being bullied, later in the book you will learn how to reduce their effect on you by creating a Power State incorporating all the things you want to feel when dealing with abusive people, such as confidence, calmness, clarity of mind, etc.

FUNDAMENTAL LESSONS & LEARNINGS...

- Emotions are actually just feelings of kinesthetic sensations in your body.
- As a verbal defender you must be aware of the sensations that tell you when you are experiencing an emotion.
- Timing plays a major role in successfully applying the skills of verbal self defense, and proper timing will be determined by your emotions.

What Are You Trying to Say?

"Nothing is so easy as to deceive oneself;
for what we wish, we readily believe."
Demosthenes

People are people wherever you go and everyone experiences their world through the same five basic senses of sight, hearing, touch, taste and smell. In fact, we all use these tools of perception so much that we stop doing it consciously and allow it to become an unconscious connection to the experiences happening all around us.

Think about that: *Doing something without paying attention to what you are doing*. Isn't that how accidents happen? I mean, you don't intentionally run into the door, stub your toe or trip on the stairs. It's simply a situation where you were not paying enough attention to what you were doing at that moment in time.

The difference between those accidents and not being aware of how you experience your interaction with another person is that it can lead to mental and emotional hurts rather than physical bumps and bruises. When you think of it that way, you can then see the possible danger in letting go of conscious control over how and what you pay attention to in another person's communication.

Even worse than not being mindful of our interaction with another person, as we grow up and lose touch with our senses, we also start blindly trusting our unconscious interpretation of another person's words and actions. Without realizing it, we lose the ability to be aware of, and adjust to, the natural changes that happen in a person over time.

As an example, just because when you first met someone and they used a certain tone of voice to express sadness it doesn't mean it will stay that way forever. Eventually, that same person may start using the same tone of voice for frustration at losing something. In time it could change to mean dissatisfaction with circumstances rather than sadness.

Generally speaking, whenever we interact with other people there is an expectation that we are going to make certain assumptions about the unspoken messages hidden in their non-verbal cues. It's simply common for people to use things like their tone of voice and facial expressions to elaborate on the deeper meaning of what they're trying to say.

An example might be the sentence, "I just got a new job." It's a short and clearly understandable statement. However, if the person says it while frowning we might assume they are unhappy about their new job. Alternatively, if the person says it with a big smile on their face we automatically assume they are pleased with their new job. In either case we are adding meaning to their words based on what we see.

Now, whenever you unconsciously make assumptions like these, you probably have no idea what sensory awareness you used to decipher the hidden message. This really won't matter too much when you're consistently right in your assumptions of other people's communication. The problem is that there are lots of communicators in this world who think they are really good at reading people and knowing what is *really* being said.

So, what do you do when you get it wrong? Everybody makes mistakes and that means it's just a fact that you are going to occasionally misinterpret other people's non-verbal communication. If you can recognize which sensory awareness gave you the wrong interpretation, then it's possible to check for clarification when there is a discrepancy. You can actually identify *how you know* what you *think you know* and then ask the person to explain what they were really trying to communicate.

Interpreting sensory awareness without confirmation is not useful because it can often lead to confusion and miscommunication, and this in turn quickly makes small problems much worse.

IMAGINE...

Imagine the following scenario where a boss interprets an employee's behavior without checking for confirmation:

USING INTERPRETATION. A boss walks into the office and looks down at the receptionist, and then suddenly stops. "What's the matter?" the boss asks.

The receptionist stops working and looks up at her quizzically and replies, "Nothing is wrong. Why do you ask?"

Shaking her head, the boss responds by saying, "No. I can tell you're annoyed about something. What is it?"

"I'm not annoyed," the receptionist says, "everything is fine."

"No, really," the boss continues, "something is annoying you. I can tell. You know it's okay if you want to talk to me about it. I'm happy to listen. What's the matter?"

Becoming more frustrated the receptionist irritably states, "Nothing is wrong. I don't know what you're talking about. I'm telling you that everything is fine."

"Okay. If you decide you want to tell me about it then you can always come and talk to me," the boss says turning and walking away.

The receptionist now sits there, angry that her boss refused to listen and frustrated by the whole experience - even though she wasn't annoyed before the exchange, she probably is now.

Using Confirmation. Now, let's replay the same scenario getting confirmation instead of just using interpretation. As the boss walks into the office she looks down at the receptionist and notices her brow is deeply furrowed. Curious to find out what's going on she stops and asks, "What's the matter?"

As the receptionist stops working she looks up and replies, "Nothing is wrong. Why do you ask?"

The boss explains, "I noticed your brow is all furrowed and your jaw looks clenched. It kinda leaves me wondering if you're annoyed about something. Is anything wrong?"

Having her physical reactions brought to her own attention, the receptionist is now forced to think about what she's feeling. After a moment of thought she looks up at her boss and simply states, "Actually, now that you mention it, the computer hasn't been working properly today and I'm a bit confused about how we're supposed deal with technical problems around here."

"Oh," with a more complete understanding, the boss smiles and says, "well we usually just call Phil down in the IT department and he'll come fix it."

With an obvious sense of relief the receptionist nods her reply, "Okay. Thanks."

Now, for some people the terms annoyed and confused might seem interchangeable but - remembering the concept of mental maps - we know that everyone has a different way of interpreting the same word. So, when the boss asked the receptionist if she was annoyed, it's possible the receptionist only applies the concept of annoyance to dealing with other people. In that case she may not have considered the computer problem as an annoyance. Instead, the receptionist may have been more concerned about making the wrong decision which she felt could lead to a reprimand. The confusion of what to do in that case would have been more likely to cause feelings of fear and anxiety rather than annoyance.

Something as simple as a single word can totally change the meaning of a statement for some people. To the person talking, it makes sense in their head, but to the listener the immediate interpretation might seem off base.

When the boss identified how she came to the conclusion that there was something wrong, it then brought it to the receptionist's attention and allowed her to determine for herself exactly what the source of the issue was. If the receptionist would have still confirmed that there was nothing wrong, then the boss would have learned that having a furrowed brow and clenched jaw was *not* a sign of a problem (at least for the receptionist anyway).

Either way, it's important to notice that during the conversation in the second example the boss was focused on understanding the receptionist's body language rather than simply validating her own perceptions.

Sensory Specific Communication

Back in 1970 a doctor by the name of Ray Birdwhistell at the University of Pennsylvania did a study called, Kinesics and Communication. Birdwhistell revolutionized the model of interpersonal communication because he discovered that only 7% of our communication is based on our choice of words while the other 93% is all non-verbal. He even went so far as to divide it further saying 38% of our communication is derived from a person's tone of voice and other vocal qualities, and the other 55% is interpreted based upon the communicator's body language.

Since most people don't really focus on how they choose to use their non-verbal communication, this means that 93% of all your communication with other people is sent and received at a completely unconscious level. Basically, a person who wants you to understand something is unconsciously sending you hints using their voice and body language as a way to help you figure out what they are getting at. All those things have a very specific meaning in their head, *but you're not in their head!*

Plus, we already know that everyone has their own interpretation of the world, and this interpretation applies to every word, every vocal component, every gesture, every facial expression and every body posture. Since the majority of our understanding is supposed to be assumed by the unconscious messages a person is sending (hidden in their voice and body language), do you think it's likely that people are going to have misunderstandings?

Hmmm... I'm sure some of you are thinking, "Well, duh! That's obvious!" So, if everyone already knows that the non-verbal parts of our interactions are totally open to interpretation, then why do people decide it must mean something hurtful? What I'm getting at is that if you're going to choose how to interpret 93% of a person's communication, why do so many people assume that the person is actually trying to make them feel bad? What if, in the other person's mind, the tone of voice they use is *not* belittling or condescending? What if, it's their way of trying to be supportive? If you are not able to actually read the other person's mind then it's entirely possible that, based on their mental map, the tone of voice they use is something their dad used for encouragement.

And yes, once more I can hear the thoughts, "But sometimes a person actually is trying to be belittling!" However, you still do not *have* to take it that way - you do have a *choice*! Just like we can misinterpret non-verbal cues negatively, we can just as easily misunderstand them to mean something positive. Truthfully, would you rather go through your day perceiving more positive experiences or more negative experiences?

Remember that you can choose to avoid attributing any specific meaning, interpretation or assumption to other people's non-verbal communication.

Even better, what if you did not apply any meaning at all? With the majority of our interpersonal communication happening unconsciously, it is best if you avoid attributing any deeper meaning, interpretation or assumption to things you see or tones you hear. In fact, it's even better if you ask for clarification when you think there is an underlying meaning to someone's message.

Whenever you think that you know what a person really means, or what they are really trying to say, that's the time it's most important to be aware of how you know those things. What exactly did you see in their facial expression or body language, or hear in the way they spoke that told you that's what they really meant?

When you recognize what that is, it's then possible for you to ask for more information about the sensory awareness you noticed.

Just like the boss in our previous example you can confirm if your understanding of an implied message is correct. Whether you're right or wrong it will give them a chance to clarify any miscommunication on their part. And, if nothing else, it will at least make them aware of how other people are interpreting their non-verbal communication.

FOR FURTHER CLARIFICATION...

USING EXTERNAL SENSORY AWARENESS

SEEING A PERSON'S PHYSIOLOGY: The old saying, "I'll believe it when I see it with my own eyes," is a simple and precise statement which shows just how important the sense of sight is in our world. With so much emphasis put towards what we see in a person's body language, it's common for people to use that visual information to add an extra dimension to their communication. We use the assumptions we make based on the person's body language to give a deeper meaning to what they are saying.

This natural instinct to combine and label our visual awareness of someone's nuances is not always useful. It can interfere with listening to our other senses. If we *see* the person as being angry then we will listen for it in their voice; so much so that we will listen until we find it, even if it's not there. Instead, look at things like body posture, components of facial expressions and hand gestures as just extra sources of knowledge, and use what you see as a point of reference when explaining yourself.

For example, be specific about your perception of their body posture by saying things like, "With your hands on your hips it seems you're...", "Leaning back and staring off into the distance makes me think you're...", "Constantly shifting your weight from foot to foot gives me the sense that you..."

With facial expressions, get as detailed as you can with things you see, such as a furrowed brow, clenched jaw or squinting eyes.

Hand gestures have many ways of being interpreted,

but they are still just physical actions. So put a description to them like, "When you're shaking your finger..." or "When you bang the table with your fist..." or "As you're wildly waving your hands in the air..." etc.

HEARING A PERSON'S INTONATIONS: The subtlest changes in things like tone, tempo and volume of someone's speech have a huge capacity to change the meaning of words. At times, the changes are so small that even the speaker is not aware they're doing it.

However, if you focus on finding different ways of describing what you hear it becomes possible to catch those changes before they influence the meaning you put to them. You want to notice if the tone of voice suddenly drops, or if the rate of speech speeds up or slows down, or if the person gets louder or quieter. When identifying changes in quality of speech you want to be aware of things like talking through clenched teeth or their voice suddenly becoming gruff or gritty.

Now, I realize that it can be difficult sometimes to give a clear description to what you hear, so when in doubt it's sometimes necessary to mimic a person's vocal qualities. This does not mean you get to mock or make fun of them; rather, this is a way to demonstrate the part of their voice that you are attempting to make reference to. Anytime you choose to demonstrate what you hear, use a non-confrontational sentence to describe it such as, "When you talk like this..." *while at the same time mimicking their vocal qualities.*

As soon as you finish that part of the sentence it's important to immediately return to your normal voice in order to explain the meaning you got from it or ask for clarification. If you continue to mimic the person's voice too long, then they will get the feeling that you are trying to poke fun at them, and that will end up turning the conversation into a confrontation.

LISTENING TO A PERSON'S WORDS: It's true that we each have our own individual meaning for the words we use. Often the difference between how two people define the same word is greater than you might imagine. For this reason, rather than rephrasing and putting things into your own words, it's much more effective to just use the exact same words they were using.

Yeah, yeah, yeah... I know - right now an entire generation of stuffy, old business men are hyperventilating after hearing that statement. Many of the business communication books and university courses used to say: "When you want to confirm there is an understanding between two people in the work place it is important that the listener paraphrase the conversation back to the speaker."

In verbal self defense that is totally the wrong thing to do! That's fine if you're just looking to ensure that you understand the person, but it's something you never want to do in times of conflict - if someone already thinks that you're not listening to them and you attempt to explain what you heard using words that they disagree with, the only thing it does is prove to the person in their own mind that you weren't paying attention.

In verbal self defense you want to avoid putting their comments in your own words as much as possible. (Remember that you're trying to utilize their mental map, not yours.) Time after time people get into big arguments because they don't think the other person understands, when in reality they're each just using a different word to explain the same thing. Believe it or not, it's possible for two people to have the same meaning for two completely different words.

Instead of risking confusion - which can cause more problems - as a good verbal defender you want to use the exact words and phrases of your attacker as much as possible (especially ones that repeat). To only use your own descriptions and explanations will leave the listener feeling even less heard and understood; however, using their words allows you to stay clear of being argumentative as you circumvent the topic of the interaction. The result is that you can keep the focus of the conversation on fixing the unacceptable, abusive behavior that you want them to stop.

When you use your external sensory awareness more effectively you can identify different components of another person's communication that bother you. As a good verbal defender, instead of choosing to take things personally, this will allow you to focus on inquiring about the other person's interpretation of their own posture, gestures, facial expressions, tone of voice, specific words and phrases, etc.

In many cases this one simple step of gaining further understanding will allow you to not feel so bullied, because when you understand the meaning the bully really intended to send you can then change how you interpret the message so it doesn't seem quite so abusive.

Bullies have a right to their opinions - they do not have a right to say and do things that leave people feeling bad.

Another terrific benefit of using sensory-specific language (describing things by the way you see, hear or feel them) is that it will help avoid escalating a confrontational situation by limiting the chances of the other person feeling judged or misunderstood. As well, it shows that you're really paying attention to them - using their words and phrases or referring to parts of their non-verbal communication will demonstrate your attentiveness.

Most importantly, always remember that when you're speaking to others using sensory-specific awareness be certain to refer to the exact sensory input that you are interpreting. For example, imagine you hear a person's tone of voice become deeper at the end of a sentence as they draw out the last few syllables. Hearing this, you might think they could be trying to belittle you and talk to you like a child. This is where you ask a question using those exact perceptions: "I noticed your tone of voice drop as you said that and it almost sounded to me like it was somewhat belittling. Did you mean it that way?"

DEVELOPING YOUR SKILLS & ABILITIES...

EXTERNAL NOTIONS OF EMOTIONS

When we're first learning to identify emotions we pick certain key elements of a person's communication that tell us what emotion we think they are experiencing. For some people it's the look in the person's eyes. For other people it might be the way the person forms their lips. Everyone will have their own unique way of identifying an emotion.

The question no one usually asks is, "How do you specifically determine what emotion someone is feeling?" Having the ability to access that information will give you an extra tool in explaining your own perceptions, plus it's useful when you want to gather more information about what the other person actually thinks they are communicating.

SET THE SCENE. Rent yourself a dramatic movie from the local video store and watch it until you find a scene where a couple of people are having an intense discussion. Preferably, find one where the communication between both people lasts for at least 30 seconds to a minute. Then watch the whole scene from start to finish a couple of times.

CONNECTING WITH A CHARACTER. While you watch the scene again, choose either one of the characters and on a piece of paper jot down all the emotions you think that person experiences during the interaction.

NOTICE HOW YOU KNEW. Whether you watch the scene again or not, list all the things that you saw and heard to support your perceptions of what the character felt. What was it about the character's communication during the scene that gave you the impression they were experiencing the emotions you just listed?

- How did their facial expression show they were feeling that emotion? Examples might be furrowed eyebrows, gritted teeth, squinting eyes, etc.
- Did they use any gestures or movements to express emotion? Examples include things like pacing, flailing their arms, banging their fist on a table, shaking their finger, etc.

- Was there anything particular about the body posture they had which gave the impression of emotions? Did their breathing affect the way you interpreted their emotions? Examples for posture would be things like hunched shoulders, head tilted to one side, hands on hips, leaning to one side or the other. Different examples of breathing might be quick, shallow, deep, a sigh, etc.
- Being aware that tone and quality of voice can be used to express emotion; did they use either of these parts of their communication to emphasize emotion? Things like ending their sentences in a high tone of voice (often used to express questions) or using a deep tone of voice to show anger. Qualities of voice will include things such as when a person's voice breaks while talking, or stuttering, or a throaty gruff sound like when someone first wakes up in the morning, etc.
- In the same way as the last two vocal components, tempo and volume of speech will easily add emotion to someone's words. Did they talk fast, slow, normal, etc.? Were they loud, quiet, normal, etc.? What words would you use to describe their voice and did it change at all during the conversation?
- Finally, write down specific words or phrases that the person used to communicate what they were feeling. Did they maybe even say what they were feeling out loud? If so, would you describe it using the same word or would you personally say they were possibly expressing a different emotion as well?

One other thing to keep in mind in situations like this is that, philosophically speaking, life isn't just a single experience - life exists as a string of experiences one after another. For that reason, every moment is directly influenced by the experiences and perceptions of the moment immediately prior to it and it directly influences the interpretation of the moment to follow. Knowing that, how much of what you decided the character was feeling is based on information you got from earlier parts of the scene?

Specifically Sensing Abusive Behaviors

If we take the time to remember that an emotion is not only a single feeling but, instead, a whole set of sensations in the body, then it becomes valuable to have a skill that allows you to sort for the sensations you specifically attribute to the emotions experienced during interpersonal conflict. As you are learning to increase your awareness of the original kinesthetic sensations behind your emotions it will become easier and easier to identify the exact moment when a feeling starts. Furthermore, developing an ability to be more aware of your negative reactions to others will allow you to better identify the specific behavior that the person is doing which is causing that reaction to begin.

> ***Bullies don't make us feel bad - bad feelings make us feel bullied.***

As a key element of being a good verbal defender this will really open your perception to what specific type of communication triggers those feelings of being bullied within you. By creating a clear understanding of what you personally consider to be mentally or emotionally abusive you will be much more effective at dealing with it.

Developing your skills & abilities…

Our Source of Suffering

Having a good ability to recognize the precise moment you begin to feel bullied is the first step of a two-step process. The next thing that needs to happen is identifying the source of those feelings by connecting your negative emotions to the bully's actual words and behaviors which are leaving you feeling that way.

Remember a Time. The way to truly identify what behaviors you consider abusive is to use real experiences from your past as point of reference. To do this you want to begin by remembering a one-time event in your past where you felt someone was treating you in an emotionally or mentally hurtful or inappropriate way. Think about what happened during the event and remember what the experience was like. What was said, how, by whom, when, where, etc.? In your mind recreate everything that happened.

GETTING THAT FEELING. While you are thinking of just this one event in your past where someone was bullying you, get a clear sense of what you felt. Focus on the sensations behind the negative emotion(s) you experienced:

- In what part of your body do you feel the sensations?
- How large or small are the feelings you sense in your body?
- Are the sensations localized to that particular part of your body? If not, is it all over, or does it move around? If it moves, is there any pattern to the way it moves through your body?
- What is the intensity of the sensation during the course of the experience?
- Are the sensations steady or do they change during the event? If they change, in what way do they change?
- Is there any sense of movement in your body? If so, in what direction(s)?
- Do you feel vibrations of any kind?
- Is there any amount of pressure or weight in, around or upon your body?
- Do you feel any particular temperature, and if so, does it change or remain constant?
- How long do the sensations last? Are the sensations constant or do they come and go?
- Is there anything else you notice about the sensations you experience?

FINDING THE SOURCE. Now that you have a deeper awareness of what sensations you experienced in your body during this event, it's time to determine what specifically the person was doing that left you feeling that way.

So, rewind your memory of this event to the beginning. Start playing it again in your mind… slowly… keep going… pay special attention to the sensations in your body. As you first begin to notice the negative sensations of your unpleasant emotion, take note of exactly when it starts and what the person is specifically doing or saying at that time (or has just finished saying or doing).

It's important to pay special attention when your feelings become more intense or unpleasant and to identify, as precisely as possible, the components of the person's communication which are making it happen. Write down on a separate sheet of paper what you notice about the person's communication that makes you feel those unpleasant things:

- Are there any specific facial expressions which create the negative feelings inside you? If so, what specific parts of their expression gave you those feelings - did they furrow their eyebrows, grit their teeth, squint, etc.?
- Did they use any hand gestures or movements that increased your feelings of being bullied? Examples could include things like threatening to hit you, banging their fist on a table, poking you in the chest, etc.
- Was there anything particular about their body posture that made you feel uncomfortable or bothered? Examples might be things like standing too close, leaning over you, head cocked to one side, hands on their hips, etc.
- Feelings of being bullied can be caused by tone and quality of voice. Did they use either of these parts of their communication to bully you? Did they incorporate things like ending their sentences in a high tone of voice to belittle your opinions or using a deep tone of voice to show aggression as part of their communication? Some bullying qualities of voice might include snarling, or snorts, or sighs, etc.

- Tempo and volume of speech can be adjusted to change the meaning of one's communication. Did they talk fast, slow, normal, etc. or did they get loud, quiet, etc. as a way to induce negative emotions in you? What words would you use to describe their voice and did they change it during the conversation?
- Were there any specific words or phrases that the person used which bothered you? Notice any words which really intensified the sensations you had of being bullied.

At this point you've probably thought about the event a few times; consider going through it once or twice more - make sure you really got everything that they were doing which made the experience so unpleasant. Once you think that you have identified all the parts of their communication you believe to be inappropriate, abusive or hurtful, you can double-check your discoveries by adjusting the way you remember the event.

Try imagining the person doing those negative behaviors or saying those inappropriate things even more and check if the feelings increase or get stronger. In the same way, if you imagine the person behaving in a different and more professional/appropriate way, does it reduce your negative feelings?

FUNDAMENTAL LESSONS & LEARNINGS...

- Growing up we lose touch with our senses and start blindly trusting our unconscious interpretation of other people's words and actions. Eventually we lose the ability to be aware of, and adjust to, the natural changes that happen in other people's idiosyncrasies and style of communication over time.
- Only 7% of our communication is based on the words we choose, while the other 93% is sent and received at a completely unconscious level - based upon tone of voice, other vocal qualities and our body language.
- Using your external sensory awareness more effectively, you can identify the specific components of a bully's communication that bother you.

So, What Do You Want From Me?

"To do a certain kind of thing, you have to be a certain kind of person."
Zen Proverb

When you can easily recognize what behaviors you consider as bullying it becomes easier to figure out how you want to deal with a bully. Trying to convince someone they're wrong or that they're intentionally hurting you will only lead to an argument. This is because a bully is just like you in the sense that they don't want to hear that they're wrong, or mean, or anything else that would leave them feeling bad.

Instead, you want to focus on the behavior as the problem (not the person) and work towards finding better alternatives. In order to achieve this, it begins with accepting the behavior that you feel is abusive as the best choice the other person has for the moment.

Then you can use relative comparisons to that behavior in order to figure out what you would prefer the person does instead.

Basically, that means, when you identify what you *don't* want the bully to say or do it will become easier to figure out what you *do* want instead. At first you can start with identifying the exact opposite behavior to what is happening and use that to generate ideas for what you're going to say rather than simply getting stuck focusing on (or worse, arguing about) why you feel the need to say it.

DEVELOPING YOUR SKILLS & ABILITIES...

CONTRAST FOR DIRECTION

There are people in this world who just seem to be natural communicators. Sometimes that's because we can connect better with those kinds of people. It's even possible that one day you might feel like you're in complete rapport with a person and the next day it's almost as if they're a different person. Comparing one day to the other the difference is not the person but rather, the *way* the person is interacting with you.

A core component of good communication is how to interact with people and that can be entirely dependent upon a multitude of different things: time and place, the situation, a person's frame of mind, etc.

This means that almost anybody can be a bully in the right circumstances. The key to remember is that, although there are a number of different variables, it's more important for us to have the ability to identify healthy communication habits rather than bad ones - that's the only way we can ask the person to use them. To generate some options of more appropriate forms of communication write down your answers to the following points on a separate piece of paper:

BAD COMMUNICATION. Go back and review your answers from the last exercise about the source of mental and emotional abuse. Go to the list of things a bully or unhealthy communicator does and says which makes you feel bullied and hurt. Specifically, things like their facial expressions, tone of voice, gestures, posture, specific words or phrases, etc.

Look at all those things that they did which bothered you, or you felt were inappropriate, in a situation you believed someone was being mentally and emotionally abusive toward you. Now choose just one of those things on the list to work with.

The Opposite of Bad Communication. Based on what you chose from the list, decide what you would prefer instead. What's a form of appropriate interaction that's opposite to the abusive tactic you listed? As an example, the opposite of yelling might be talking in a pleasant tone of voice. For using profanity the opposite might be to refrain from using profanity.

Now go through the rest of the abusive bullying communication tactics you feel are inappropriate and define a preferred, opposite, healthy behavior for each. Determine how specifically you want the person to behave or talk.

Along with having a more detailed understanding of what kind of communication you require in order to remove any feelings of being bullied, you can now directly ask for it using sensory specific detailed behavior. Remember that people need clear instructions to follow if you want them to do something. If you provide the person with specific directions for an alternative behavior to do in place of their bullying behavior it will increase your chances of getting them to change the way they interact with you.

IMAGINE...

In older movies it was common for police officers to yell "FREEZE!" when they went to arrest the bad guy. However, this particular command falls short of being very specific, even if the only thing the officer wants is for the criminal to cease their current action/behavior.

The actual goal of a law enforcement officer is to arrest the bad guy, which basically means *to subdue and detain the person*. For a police officer to do this efficiently and effectively, new directions with more specific outcomes would be required.

When the officer yelled "FREEZE!" the criminal might have stopped running, but that did not necessarily reduce their hostility or put them in a more compliant position. Today, law enforcement officers yell more directive instructions such as, "Stop! Stop moving! Lay face-down on the ground! Spread your arms and legs wide. Stop talking. Hold still."

By being more specific in this way the criminal has sensory specific instructions which are clear, easy to understand, simple to follow and lead to an outcome where the police officer has greater control of the situation. In the same way, you must give a bully specific behaviors you want them to do.

When your directions are too general and ambiguous it leaves the interpretation of your words in the hands of your listener, and that may not match your expectations. Telling a bully, "Stop being so rude," allows them to define what rude behaviors are. Instead, you need specifics such as, "I'd really appreciate it if you'd please look at me while we talk."

So, make certain that the healthy behavior you prefer is described in sensory specific language (an explanation that identifies what you'll see, hear or feel). As much as possible avoid telling them what you don't want and try to rephrase it as how you want them to treat you. Instead of telling someone to, "stop being rude," explain what you mean by asking them to act differently. An example might be to say, "Please refrain from interrupting me when I'm speaking," which provides clear instructions for what you want.

One of the main benefits of being able to directly tell people how you would like them to treat you is that you can consider whether or not you are using it in times of conflict. It's a simple fact that all humans make mistakes from time to time and you're a human, so that includes you as well. The point now is that you know what to look for in order to identify a good communicator. This allows you to catch yourself when you get caught up in the conflict before you lose control of your emotions and do or say (or *not* do or say) something you will regret.

This also means that the next time you're having trouble communicating with someone it might be a good idea to get curious about any negative components of your own way of interacting with them. Try taking the other person's point of view for a moment and check to see that you are using the qualities of healthy communication that you expect from others.

My Behaviors, My Values

In the first chapter we learned that the real purpose behind our negative emotions (including feelings of being bullied) is to highlight problems which our unconscious mind believes we should put our attention toward solving. Negative emotions are simply unconscious spotlights directing our attention toward deeper values that are being violated. Those are the things which are important to us about who we see ourselves to be, and how we believe life should work, often defined in terms of right or wrong, and good or bad. In most self-help literature found in our local book stores these deeper values are commonly referred to as our *personal boundaries.*

By recognizing that the deeper meaning behind an emotion is about what we personally value, it highlights how important it is for us to be aware of what specifically our emotions are trying get us to focus on. These deep personal values are actually the main element of any behavioral process, including bullying. They're what provide the underlying sense of motivation which triggers those unconscious decisions we make. Our deeper values actually supply the unconscious reason of why we do what we do, and why we say what we say.

As you may remember, the unconscious process of how people choose what they do or say is supposed to achieve a higher purpose. The behavioral output of a person is the way their unconscious mind thinks it will achieve the person's deeper value or get their basic needs met.

The interesting benefit of knowing this little secret is that we, as verbal defenders, can then recognize that there are dozens of different behaviors which will accomplish the same higher positive intention. This allows us to open our awareness to looking for different options of what to do or say that will; 1) meet our deeper value(s) while, at the same time; 2) be acceptable to the other person(s) involved.

In the situation where an office bully is being abusive, by using sensory awareness to notice the negative feelings in your body you have the ability to realize it as soon as it starts to bother you. At that point you can identify which specific behavior the person is doing that you feel is most inappropriate or abusive. The next step is to figure out why it's such a big deal for you and what deeper value is being violated by their bullying behavior?

In order to figure this out you want to think of what the opposite behavior is that you would prefer they do and then determine the value of that desired behavior. So, if someone is yelling and it bothers you, first determine the opposite behavior. In this example we will pretend the opposite is talking in a pleasant tone of voice.

Then you want to know what the higher purpose of talking in a pleasant tone of voice is. What makes that so important to you? When you discover that deeper value behind talking in a pleasant tone of voice then you have the power to be flexible in finding options the other person will do that don't cause you to feel bullied.

IDENTIFYING MY VALUES

When you are trying to understand what the higher purpose is of a behavior, the most useful way to think of those underlying personal values is to consider them like categories which represent your personal morals, ethics and principles. An individual behavior is merely one external way to represent or show a particular moral or principle. It's important to take note that every behavior can represent more than one deeper value depending upon the situation. As an example, talking in a pleasant tone of voice can demonstrate several values such as kindness, respect, professionalism, etc.

> ***The more flexible you choose to be, the more options you have for dealing with a bully.***

In order to determine the connection between the form of healthy communication you desire and the deeper value it represents, ask yourself, "What good quality or personal characteristic is this preferred behavior an example of?"

So, if we ask, "What personal quality or characteristic is 'talking to someone in a pleasant tone of voice' an example of?" some answers might include: "having respect for others;" "being a nice person;" or, "being professional." All of these describe a deeper value and higher purpose that can be demonstrated through many different behaviors, not just talking to someone in a pleasant tone of voice.

After you have discovered the deeper value or higher intention of the behavior you want, you can then increase your flexibility in how" to get what you want by looking for more options. If the person you are dealing with is unable or unwilling to 'talk in a pleasant tone of voice' then think of other ways he/she can communicate with you in a way that meets your deeper value of that behavior (i.e. having respect for others; being a pleasant person; or, interacting in a professional manner). You might consider options such as, using a quieter volume, communicating through email and memos, talking to each other less often, etc. Remember that you may not always get what you want but, if you choose to be flexible, you can always find a way to get whatever you need/value.

FOR FURTHER CLARIFICATION…

THE FREEDOM OF BEING MORE FLEXIBLE

If someone says, "You need to learn to be more flexible," the two questions that often come in response are; 1) "Why?" and 2) "What do you actually mean by flexible?"

Well… those are good questions and I'm glad you asked… you see, the reason for wanting to be flexible is best summarized by the *Law of Requisite Variety,* which is a fundamental component of understanding human behaviors. Originally this law was based on something called Systems Theory and we can generalize its interpretation for verbal self defense by defining it as; "The person with the most flexibility will have the most influence in the relationship."

What this basically means is that a person who is more willing to adjust the way in which they can get their needs met is most likely to feel fulfilled (to feel like they are getting what they want.) So, an actual example of being more flexible might be if you want someone to understand you, then, by being open to different options of how you are willing to communicate with that person, you are guaranteed to find a way of explaining yourself which works for the way they need to understand it.

In the same sense, the more flexible you are in how an abusive person can be more respectful or polite (or whatever the deeper value is that you want from them), the greater your chance is of finding something that works for both of you.

Now, I realize that for some people it may not always seem like you can think of other options; however, those are merely the limitations of your mental map. The more flexible you choose to be, the more options you can offer a bully for how they could change their behavior to be less abusive. This way it still allows them to feel they have a choice rather than being forced to do something different. As well, it helps to take your focus off the feelings their abusive behavior is creating inside you and, instead, focuses your awareness on finding a solution that will create a positive working environment for everyone - the less attention you give feelings of being bullied, the less power those feelings will have over your life.

DEVELOPING YOUR SKILLS & ABILITIES...

STRETCHING FOR MORE FLEXIBILITY

IDENTIFY ABUSIVE COMMUNICATION. Take a moment to remember all the different ways people have treated you that left you feeling bad. Now, take a piece of paper and write out in as much detail as possible one of the ways you think an abusive person could interact with someone that would cause them to feel bad.

As much as possible, use sensory specific language such as description of their body posture, tone of voice, specific words they would use, facial expressions, etc. that make the person they are talking to feel bullied.

DEFINE THE OPPOSITE. What healthy communication tactic is opposite to the abusive behavior you just described in the previous question? How would someone prefer to be treated instead? Again, use sensory specific descriptions about their body posture, tone of voice, specific words they would use, facial expressions, etc.

CREATE FLEXIBILITY. Think about the positive communication tactic you defined in the question above and then consider what deeper value you think that behavior is an example of? What good quality or personal characteristic is this positive behavior an example of? What kind of person talks to and interacts with someone in that manner?

Now describe 3 other ways you can communicate with someone that demonstrates this deeper value. What specific things do you do or say when talking or working with other people to show you have that personal quality and that you are that kind of person?

Keep in mind that the more choices of healthy communication tactics (specific words and behaviors) that you can come up with which will alleviate your sense of being bullied, the greater the likelihood is that you will find one that a bully is going to be willing to agree to.

THEIR BEHAVIORS, THEIR VALUES

Since we know that all your behaviors have a deeper value or higher positive intention, then it's fair to assume every behavior that everyone else does has a higher positive intention too. In the same way that all this applies to you, it equally applies to the office bullies you meet along the way. The difference is that their words and behaviors are each driven by their own deeper values - not yours.

IMAGINE...

For an example of the deeper value which drives a bullying behavior we can look at one possible reason why some bullies are so mentally and emotionally abusive:

Verbal abuse (as well as non-verbal abuse) is a complex behavior, and the reason behind it is most likely different for every person in every individual situation. For ease of explanation we are going to set the scene as a boss being verbally abusive in the context of an office environment.

Now, one possible underlying reason which drives his behavior could be a deeper need for recognition of his authority. This is just one of thousands of possible unconscious reasons, but it's the one we are going to use just for this example. So, let's assume he highly values *respect for one's superiors* and consequently he believes that it should be just as important to everyone else too.

In situations where he is not treated in a way which he perceives in his mental map as respectful he might become annoyed, frustrated, or angry. When these negative emotions build up they might cause him to occasionally act like a bully by yelling and using profanity towards his staff.

Even though the bullying behavior of yelling and using profanity is motivated by his deeper need for staff to treat him with respect, he acts that way unconsciously and it's completely outside his awareness. For this reason he is merely reacting to what he perceives as inappropriate behavior on their part.

Believe it or not, this boss may never actually be aware that how he's acting himself is exactly what he wants his staff *not* to do. He's treating them the way he hopes they do not treat him! (Definitely not a case of lead by example here.)

What makes it even more difficult for him to realize that he's being a bully is the fact that he only focuses on addressing each individual source of frustration as it comes up. A single misfiled document might trigger an abusive tirade from the boss but it's not the real problem. His deeper value of showing respect for one's superiors is what he's actually trying to achieve, but instead he simply focuses on aggressively dealing with the trigger. The result is that he'll get angry and demand better performance from his staff when they're handling documents, but this is just one example of the deeper issue.

What he really needs is more daily interactions with his staff that fulfill his sense of being shown respect for his authority - only then will his bullying behavior go away on its own. Since he doesn't realize this fact, he is unable to put company policies and procedures in place that will meet his deeper values in a more appropriate way. The end result will be on going office bullying on his part, leading to a high employee turn-over rate which only exacerbates the problem and negatively impact the company's bottom line.

No Excuses

For everyone who is thinking right now, "*OMG! Are you really going to try and justify a bully's behavior*?!" my answer is: No. I am not condoning what the boss does in this example - I am simply pointing out that there is a deeper value and higher positive intention behind every behavior.

If the boss feels that his subordinates are not treating him fairly - much like a person who is being bullied feels they are not being treated fairly - then it might be more useful for him to read this book and learn to identify the deeper value behind what he wants. That way, he could put forward options to his staff in a more appropriate and professional manner.

One example might be for him to, instead of yelling and being abusive, ask for what he wants from them in a way that he's more likely to get it - as my grandma used to say, "You'll always catch more flies with honey than with vinegar." The first step, however, is for him to recognize there is a deeper value behind his bullying behaviors and a higher positive intention to what he wants from his employees. Only then can he find alternate ways of getting those needs met.

Verbal Self Defense is NOT Persuasion

Although you now have a better understanding of how behaviors are driven by deeper values, it's best to avoid trying to work with other people's values when using verbal self defense. The communications tactics used in identifying what someone wants and then working towards finding out why that is so important to them are more in line with effective persuasion skills rather than verbal defensive tactics. Finding a way to allow the other person to achieve their higher positive intention in a way that also works within the guidelines of your deeper values is the foundation of Behavioral Persuasion (an incredibly valuable skill which requires a whole book of its own to properly explain).

The concern is that if you do not already have healthy communication with someone then techniques for persuasion will not necessarily change that. In order to be able to persuade someone to think differently and be open to options they must be willing to communicate with you appropriately - they must be already open to listening and interacting with you in positive ways. Abusive communicators and office bullies are not usually open to talking about their deeper values to begin with, so attempting to use behavioral persuasion tactics will be somewhat useless.

FOR FURTHER CLARIFICATION...

LIMITS OF BEHAVIORAL PERSUASION

The problem with trying to be persuasive in situations of bullying is that the real issue of their mentally and emotionally abusive words and actions will be outside the topic of discussion. In order for you to be free to persuade another person to think or act differently it requires the communication between the two of you to be genuine and free of negative emotions - only then is behavioral persuasion possible.

However, a great verbal defender can still choose to go beyond simple verbal self defense by at least taking into consideration the mental and emotional safety of your attacker while you're defending your own right to be treated appropriately and professionally. To do this it's a matter of always controlling your own communication in order to be certain you're avoiding comments that would discount or disregard the bully's opinions, feelings and perceptions.

As one example, it's okay if they want to be treated with respect but it's not okay for them to yell and use profanity in an attempt to get it. In reverse, you have a right to verbally defend yourself from such behaviors but it's not useful to label the person as mean, selfish, or stupid for acting that way. So, to keep your attacker mentally and emotionally safe you simply need to refrain from referring to their behavior in those ways - when communicating with a bully it's best to simply refrain from placing judgment on them or their bullying behaviors.

FUNDAMENTAL LESSONS & LEARNINGS...

- Beyond the obvious benefit of being able to directly tell a bully how you would prefer they treat you, another benefit of knowing what you perceive as healthy communication is that you can consider whether or not you are using it in times of conflict.
- As a good verbal defender you want to be specific when asking a bully to adjust the offensive components of their communication. Describing exactly what behavior you want reduces the chance for misinterpretations.
- Deep personal values are actually the main element which is the motivation behind any behavior, including bullying.
- To increase your chance of success, develop an ability to look for multiple options of what you want from the bully that will still fit within your deeper values.
- Remember that the person with the most flexibility will have the most influence in the relationship.
- The more choices for healthy communication tactics (specific words and behaviors) that you can come up with which will alleviate your sense of being bullied, the greater the likelihood is that you will find one the bully is willing to agree to.
- The main problem with trying to use techniques of persuasion in situations of bullying is that the real issue of mentally and emotionally abusive words and actions is not the main topic of discussion. Verbal self defense focuses on fixing the abusive behaviors so that a civilized discussion will be possible.

PART IV

CONTROL YOUR SELF

Prior to the 1960s the mind and body were considered two separate entities. What went on in mind affected the mind, and what went on in body remained in the body. In the 1970s there was more of a connection between mind and body and, eventually, it generally became accepted that the mind-body separation is a more scientific model and the mind-body connection is a more humanistic model.

In verbal self defense we adhere to the humanistic model of the mind-body connection because anything that is emotionally felt in the body will affect the mind and, in the same way, thoughts of the mind will affect the body. We can consider the concept of fear as a clear example of how direct this mind-body connection truly is.

You can get a sense of this when you imagine someone who is expected to do a public presentation but suffers from a phobia of public speaking. When the mind dwells on the perception of possible failure in the future event, this causes sensations of tension and anxiety in the body. That anxiousness only feeds the fear of failure even further creating a cycle between the mind and body, each feeding off the other, to create stress about the person's up-coming presentation.

So, the physiological sensations of the emotion effects how the mind creates specific perceptions of the event, which only makes the person even more aware of the physical sensations of the emotion.

Different components of verbal self defense utilize this principle that the mind and body are connected. In the same way that negative feelings create negative thoughts, which in turn create more negative feelings, the reverse is also true. Positive changes in the body can bring about positive shifts in the mind, and that will increase positive feelings in the body. So, changing your mind will change your physiology in the same way that changing your physiology will change your mind.

USING THE MIND-BODY CONNECTION

The most obvious external output of one's mind-body connection is commonly referred to as a person's mental or emotional state or their State of Mind. It's comprised of the ongoing mental (Mind) and physiological (Body) conditions within them and it's simply the person's way of being in the moment.

People are constantly changing states unconsciously from one moment to the next based on what is happening around and within them, almost seemingly without control. However, even though events in the external world may seem to influence our specific state at any moment in time (i.e. someone or something may seem to *make* us happy or sad), we are still the only ones who are solely responsible for which state we choose to be in. Believe it or not, you actually have the ability to change your state with volition. In NLP it's believed that we are each in charge of our minds, and therefore our results.

This has far-reaching implications for how we learn, how we affect others and how successful we are in the world. This is because the state you are in is not the same as experiencing an event in itself; rather, your state is how you react to the experiences in that event. So, how you react to a bully depends greatly upon your state of mind.

When you have more flexibility (more choice) in what your state is, or will be, you have more emotional freedom. It will also give you access to a variety of emotional responses to any particular situation - simply by changing how you are thinking about that situation. You can shift how you are using your body and how you are using your mind by making yourself aware of different sensation in your body and then focusing your mind on thinking and acting differently. The end goal will eventually be to develop greater control over how you emotionally respond to bullying in any form or context.

FAKE IT UNTIL YOU MAKE IT

In times of stress and difficulty it's easy to become unsure, confused and fearful. For a verbal defender to use their skills successfully they must have an ability to conceive themselves as being successful. This is where we turn to Hans Vaihinger's 1911 paper *Philosophie des Als Ob* (Philosophy of As If).

Vaihinger asserted that the simple act of, "pretending that you are competent at something," will allow you to overcome any perceived limitations or emotional resistance to doing it. This way of thinking makes it easier to explore possibilities and ideas which would not usually be available to you due to limiting beliefs about yourself or the situation.

Using your awareness of the sensation in your body and focusing on thinking and acting differently can help control your emotional response to bullying.

The goal then is to use Vaihinger's theory to temporarily remove your limiting beliefs and perceptions so that you can explore other options. Combined with state of mind you can soon discover more useful ways of controlling how you mentally and emotionally react to bullying.

KEEPING BALANCE IN MIND

"Balance is key: I need to be successful in my career to feel fulfilled, be surrounded by people I care about to share it with, and have my health to be able to do the things I love to do!"
Kiana Tom

The behavior of children in our community is one of the purest glimpses into the kind of people we are. Their thoughts and actions are natural and free of hidden intentions. Kids just react to their inner perceptions by doing and saying the things they have learned from watching the adults around them.

One of the most interesting observations we can bring attention to is the fact that no one likes to be left out. Nobody wants to be that person who does not get a piece of cake at the party, who does not have a place to sit at the table, who does not get a turn on the swing, etc. Although it's true that psychologists like to study how a child reacts to this kind of treatment, the thing we should be focusing on is the fact that children on any playground in the world want to make sure they get the same as everyone else. Anything less and they will call it like they see it - it's unfair.

This deep need for fairness and balance can be seen all around us: the Scales of Justice in our legal system; the goal of a Balanced Budget for our government; doctors commonly say that a seriously ill patient's life, "Hangs in the Balance;" Yin and Yang in Chinese medicine; the endless number of Olympic events requiring balance and poise; mentally ill people are said to be unbalanced; etc.

A State of Imbalance

Workplace bullying is one more place where that sense of balance is in play. Victims of bullies will often talk about being treated unfairly and, in fact, this applies to any situation of conflict.

Truthfully, martial artists have known the importance of this concept for thousands of years. Students of martial arts such as Aikido and Judo are always looking to take away their opponent's balance in order to win a battle. This allows a person to be in control of the fight by controlling their opponent's ability to move. It's often this sense of control and power that playground bullies are looking for when they pick on smaller children - and the nature of office bullies is exactly the same.

Workplace bullies are simply looking to knock people down in a different way. They want to knock them mentally and emotionally off balance. Whether it's a conscious intention or not, behaviors of workplace bullying are designed to allow the bully to get their way by having the victim feel powerless.

Occasionally you will see it both as a mental and physiological response in the person being bullied. When an office bully strikes, some victims will go so far as to lean their body away from their attacker (putting themselves physically off balance). In other cases you will hear the victim stutter and fumble to find the right words as they try to think of what to say (having been thrown mentally off balance). Both of these are examples of how important it is for a verbal defender to maintain his or her balance.

The Emotional Response

When a bully first attacks it will generate an emotional response. As the attacker says or does something that directly violates your personal values and beliefs about how you expect to be treated, it will create a negative emotion.

Minor issues are often handled by the logical part of our mind, while violations of deeper and more important values are more commonly addressed by the emotional part of our mind. This is because the more important the issue is to us, the more intense the emotion will be.

Small emotional responses can be handled with a level-head. When we're more upset it feels like it's much more important for us to defend ourselves because the negative emotion is so overpowering.

No one likes to feel bad so, when we feel real bad, that unpleasant emotion becomes the main filter of our mind. It's all our unconscious mind wants us to focus on until it can be dealt with. The problem is that an emotionally focused mind is not useful for making good decisions. When our choice of behavior is driven by our emotions, putting those emotions in control of thoughts and actions, we can often do or say things that are inappropriate.

The reason is because an emotionally focused mind is only interested in short term solutions. It only seeks immediate gratification and reprieve from the strong negative feelings. When someone makes impulsive decisions it may have positive short term results but have even worse negative long term consequences.

In comparison, during happy times the emotionally focused mind can have a great value. It's what allows us to connect good feelings to healthy behaviors, provides us with motivation and adds passion to our life. It's the connection to those good emotions which are the spice of life, making things enjoyable, keeping us going when doing those hard tasks and fighting for what we believe in. The issue for us is, when we're in situations of being bullied, an emotionally focused mind will only hinder us from using our verbal self defense skills effectively.

The Logical Response

In contrast to having an emotionally focused mind, we can also have a logically focused mind. Sometimes people can even go to an extreme and simply shut down and feel nothing. When someone is disconnected from any emotional connection to life it can create a very logical way of thinking - and take note that this doesn't mean the person is any more sensible than before, it simply means they can systematically rationalize their way through a problem without any emotional input.

The logically focused mind is usually calm and rational and it's easy to maintain when everything feels fine. This is the kind of mental focus that is required in order to think clearly and determine the best choices which will produce the most long term gain. This particular frame of mind is also very useful for following instructions.

Any options created by a logically focused mind are driven by reason and work mostly with the facts of the situation. This is because the logical mind is analytical in nature and, therefore, good for planning and problem solving.

The limitation comes with the fact that we require emotion for motivation in order to avoid over-analyzing things. The logically focused mind has a tendency to think too much and often leaves people unfeeling, uncaring and bland about life.

IMAGINE…

Imagine you were riding your bike down the road and, for whatever reason, you lost control, hit the curb, and flew over the handlebars. Then suppose the impact of striking the pavement caused you to injure your shoulder and cut open your forehead.

When you get to the hospital, what would you think if the emergency room doctor turns to look at you and, when he does, his face goes white, he gasps in shock, bursts into tears, crying, "Oh God! Oh God! What are we going to do?" Would his reaction give you a sense of confidence and make you feel calm and reassured? I would wager most people's answer is: No.

Emergency room staff, Ambulance EMT, Firefighters, Police, Military and any other emergency rescue personnel in our society are trained to control their emotions. The reason is because we do not want them making illogical and emotionally charged decisions.

All of these people have very important jobs to do, and those jobs are well structured with specific step-by-step procedures that have been proven to be the most successful at saving lives. This system of logically determined responses helps to ensure that you get the best results possible when you find yourself in any kind of serious, life threatening situation.

The alternative is much less desirable. I mean, do you really want a police officer, who carries a gun on the job, to lose his temper and get angry before he makes a decision? The answer is definitely: No.

(So, the next time you have to deal with people in law enforcement, please allow them a little understanding. Remember that, although they may seem rude, uncaring and cold, the truth is that they are simply trained to do their job without letting any emotions - good or bad - get involved.)

THE BALANCED RESPONSE

Somewhere between our logical style of thinking and our emotional reactions to life is a balanced mind. This is our ability to take into account the logical understanding and important components of the situation or experience, while also addressing the emotional need to have our personal thoughts and beliefs validated.

A balanced mind gives you the ability to act with confidence, certainty and a sense of knowing.

What that means is logic and emotions are both equally integrated in the balanced mind. This is the mental state where you have a sense of being steady and grounded in your principles, and still able to maintain the freedom and flexibility to choose different options of how to respond.

A fully balanced mind is commonly experienced as a quiet stillness and peaceful tranquility inside, allowing you to remain true to yourself along with feeling validated in your decision. This deep sense of balance and calmness helps you let negative emotions pass through you without any residual effects. You can logically take any lesson and learning gained from an experience while more easily letting go of the negative emotions connected to it. All together a balanced mind gives you the ability to act with confidence, certainty and a sense of knowing.

CENTER OF BALANCE

At this point it's important to recall the mind-body connection and how they affect one another. It's through that deeper connection we recognize our physical balance and mental balance are inextricably related. This means that when you take a physically balanced position your mind comes into balance as well. Likewise, if your body is off balance, reaching a balanced state of mind will help you to regain your equilibrium.

The problem after that is in maintaining that balance in the midst of conflict - that will take practice. In order to practice we turn to the teachings of Aikido. In the Japanese marital art of Aikido the concept of balance is often referred to as Centering, which is the act of achieving balance in mind and body.

DEVELOPING YOUR SKILLS & ABILITIES…

CENTERING MIND AND BODY

A human being's physiological center is commonly considered to be a person's *Center of Gravity*. It's the spot where your weight reaches its maximum concentration and balance, achieving equilibrium between the upper and lower part of the body. At this physical center of your body is the powerful pelvic structure in which your balance is cradled, allowing you to stand erect and keep a relaxed, upright posture continuously with relative ease.

FINDING YOUR CENTER. To find your center begin by imagining the one point where your three center lines intersect - the center lines between the left and right side of your body, front and back of your body and upper and lower part of your body. This point will be your *physiological center.*

To first experience your center, start by lying down on your back in a relaxed state. Let yourself get into a symmetrical, relaxed posture and notice your breathing slow down as it regulates itself.

From there, put your hand on your abdomen directly above where you imagined your physiological center point to be. Concentrate on this spot inside your body - imagine all your focus and all your energy is going to that spot.

When you get the sense that your focus has arrived in your center, concentrate on keeping it there. When you are fully centered you should feel your muscles relax even further. You might also notice a sensation of warmth spreading through your body.

Practice locating and holding your center for a few minutes, 3 times a day for a week. As you get more comfortable with this exercise begin to find and hold your center without the use of your hand. Simply concentrate on the spot, feel it warm up as you get into it, and hold it.

Be mindful of staying centered. If you find your mind slipping off into other thoughts, avoid any feelings of concern. Keep bringing your attention back to centering yourself and you will soon find those interruptions will be fewer and fewer.

MAINTAINING YOUR CENTER. The next step is to begin finding and holding center while sitting and standing. The process is the same except there are more distractions than when you were lying down.

Start by centering yourself while sitting. Sit in a symmetrical, relaxed posture and imagine your center point has real weight to it as you lower your concentration to that point. Feel yourself get heavier, with a sensation of sinking into the chair.

When you're ready, try to center yourself while standing. Stand in a balanced, symmetrical posture with your feet shoulder width apart and your arms resting at your sides. Find a comfortable position with your weight evenly distributed and your knees slightly bent. When you're in a comfortable posture, repeat the centering process - lower your concentration to your center and focus your breathing there.

Take the time to practice centering yourself sitting or standing for a few minutes, 3 times a day, for a week. Remember to be mindful of holding your center and keeping your breathing relaxed.

After you have gained some experience in centering yourself you can begin holding it while moving. You can discover how you would stay centered while walking, playing sports, dancing or even riding on the bus. When you do this it's useful to imagine that you are moved by your center rather than you are moving your center.

Try it walking down the street some time. Imagine that your center is moving and the rest of your body is being supported and carried along by your center. With practice you will very quickly discover that you have better balance, posture and move more smoothly as you walk.

At first you may exaggerate the movements by pushing your center out ahead of yourself. In time, when you are doing it right, you will find your normal gait. Just by holding your center in daily life you will discover people start treating you better and showing you more respect.

Then, when you find it necessary to deal with conflict or bullying you will be less likely to mentally (or physically) get knocked off balance and forced into submission. Instead, even if you are caught off guard, you will much more quickly regain your balance and maintain control of yourself, your thoughts and your actions.

FUNDAMENTAL LESSONS & LEARNINGS...

- Workplace bullies are looking to knock people off balance mentally and emotionally so they can control the person and the situation in order to get what they want.
- Keeping your balance is the first step in staying in control of yourself.
- Balance your body and your mind will follow. Balance your mind and your body will follow.

STATE... WHAT YOU WANT

"The greatest revolution of our generation is the discovery that human beings, by changing the inner attitudes of their minds, can change the outer aspects of their lives."
William James

The basic premise for human behavior is that the human brain executes certain programs or strategies in order to accomplish pre-determined tasks or expected outcomes. A key element of behavioral modification coaching is that it relies a great deal on being able to recognize, utilize and shift the mental and emotional patterns of perception which influence a person's choice of behavior - if you change how you mentally and/or emotionally perceive a situation you will alter how you react to it.

The main concern is that one's state of mind is what holds the majority of influence over our ability to properly perceive and interact in any given situation. Whether your performance will be mediocre or excellent is going to be greatly impacted by the mental and emotional state you are in at that moment in time because they are what control a great deal of your mental filters.

This means that the efficacy and effectiveness of a person's response in situations of bullying largely depends on what state of mind they take on during the experience. We know this because the mind and body affect each other, so any negative physiological responses will decrease your mental effectiveness and emotional control. Meaning your level of stress, heart rate, breathing rate, body posture, blood pressure, tension, etc. can ultimately determine how well you are able to use your verbal self defense skills when you need them most.

This is why Olympic athletes who are preparing for an event put so much emphasis on preparing themselves mentally, not just physically - it's very important that they have a strong ability to remain calm, relaxed and focused during their event, and this is accomplished by controlling their state of mind.

Now, the first step in controlling your state of mind is to be able to recognize and monitor your own internal states. This ability to identify your own state and notice state shifts in yourself is an extremely valuable skill, and by making yourself aware of the patterns and cues that influence your internal state you can increase the degree of choice you have in responding to workplace bullying.

The Mental State of Being Bullied

There are a lot of different negative emotions people commonly feel when being bullied, and none of them are useful for self defense. In fact, from the moment of being pushed mentally off balance things can begin to spiral out of control.

Once a negative emotion begins to arise our body keeps responding with more and more unpleasant feelings. Those feelings work against us by stealing our attention and making it more difficult to respond effectively. When this happens we can feel even worse, resulting in a further increase of unpleasant sensations. Back and forth the cycle can continue until finally the whole event ends leaving us feeling mentally and emotionally abused and often obsessing about going back and handling it differently - wishing we could go back and re-do the event being more prepared to deal with or work around those unpleasant feelings.

So, negative emotions brought on by situations of conflict only work to filter our perceptions for more negative awareness. The reason for this is that the negative state of mind created by being bullied makes us focus more and more on the negative, unpleasant parts of the situation; such as our inability to have a positive impact on controlling the moment, or even controlling ourselves.

MANAGING YOUR STATE OF MIND. Rather than being swept up by the negative emotional response of the situation, it's much more useful to choose the state of mind you want and have access to it when you need it. This means you need to build the verbal defender state of mind which will be most effective for helping you deal with bullies.

In order to do this you first need to know how to manage your internal state. Only then can you begin to pick and choose when and how you will emotionally respond to situations of conflict and abuse.

This is accomplished by using the mind-body connection to reconnect with significant emotional states from our past. In this way, internal states can be recalled and utilize at any particular moment in order for us to be more effective.

DEVELOPING YOUR SKILLS & ABILITIES...

ACCESSING A STATE OF MIND

Accessing a specific internal state requires you to establish a cue or trigger for the desired state. In order to do this you must first choose the state you want to access.

Begin by choosing a useful state of mind that you would like to be able to have any time you choose. Some examples of states such as these include things like: calmness, confidence, courage, mental clarity, openness, etc. Pick the one you want to use in this exercise and then follow the steps below:

STEP 1: RECALL THE STATE. Remember a one-time event in your past when you experienced the desired state. In many instances you will be experiencing more than a single state of mind. In this case, pick a past event where the main state you experienced was the desired state.

STEP 2: RECOVER THE STATE. Now, in your mind, go back and relive that event. Remember everything that happened and re-experience it all over again - see things through your own eyes, hearing through your own ears and feeling the sensations throughout your entire body (including things like your rate of breathing).

Continue this process going through the memory over and over again until you can recover all the physiological sensations, movements, postures, muscle tension, etc. that induce the state fully and completely. Really be certain you can get the sense of what it was totally like to be in that specific state of mind.

STEP 3: CONNECT THE STATE. When you have fully and completely got the full sensation of being in the desired state of mind again, take a breath and simply say to yourself, "I am absolutely [*INSERT THE NAME OF YOUR DESIRED STATE HERE*]!" Be sure you make this statement with absolute confidence and conviction as you fully and completely sense what it's like to be in that state.

STEP 4: LET GO. Now take a moment to shake it off. Release all the tension in your muscles and sensations in your body - just think about random things for a moment feeling nothing in particular until you have completely let go of the state you were in.

STEP 5: MAKE IT AUTOMATIC. At this point repeat steps 1-4 with the same state of mind until you can easily and effortlessly access that state at will. Eventually you will find that you can simply take a breath and say to yourself, "I am absolutely [*INSERT THE NAME OF YOUR DESIRED STATE HERE*]!" and it will trigger you to unconsciously take on that desired state of mind automatically.

In order to really install the ability to access this state at will, you can practice inducing the state by saying the sentence at 3 random times a day for a week.

Creating Your Power State

When dealing with abusive people we already know that it will leave you feeling bad in some way if you are mentally or emotionally knocked off balance. So the next step is to build yourself a Power State which you can utilize when dealing with workplace bullies.

The key to doing this is to recognize that when you access a specific state of mind even very subtle physiological changes can affect your ability to maintain that desired state. In order to optimize the effectiveness of your preferred state you want to be aware of any subtle cues that will allow you to more fully experience that desired state consciously.

Since bullying behaviors have a negative impact on your mental and emotional state, they will induce physiological responses which can reduce your effectiveness at verbally defending yourself. Although, accessing and working from a more useful state of mind can help, the process of holding that positive state can be interrupted if the negative feelings caused by being bullied are stronger than the state of mind you are trying to maintain.

In order to ensure your verbal self defense is effective and that you are able to maintain control your Power State must be stronger than any possible negative emotions created by a bullying experience. As a way to make certain that your Power State is stronger than any potential negative reactions you could have from being bullied, it's necessary to use more than just one desired state. In fact, you should have at least 5 different resourceful states of mind which can be combined in order to create a really, really strong power state for yourself.

DEVELOPING YOUR SKILLS & ABILITIES...

BUILDING YOUR POWER STATE

After experiencing situations of bullying, people are often left feeling bad in some way. Consequently we often think about all the things we wish we could have said or done in those situations instead.

The real question at this point then is: "What state of mind would you need to be in so you could have handled the situation better?"

STEP 1: CHOOSE 5 RESOURCE STATES. Listed below are a number of different states that are considered by many to be useful in times of conflict. Go through the list and choose five (5) that you believe would be the most useful for you when verbally defending yourself. There have been a few blanks left in case you think of other states you would prefer.

□ Confidence	□ Calm	□ Creative
□ Focused	□ Competent	□ Courageous
□ Energetic	□ Peaceful	□ Joyous
□ Understanding	□ Open	□ Curious
□ Resourceful	□ Aware	□ Strong
□ Self-Assured	□ Knowledgeable	□ Tactful
□ Diplomatic	□ Professional	□ Suave
□ Regal	□ Gracious	□ Charming
□ Considerate	□ Friendly	□ Humble
□ Jovial	□ Pleasant	□ Relaxed
□ Self-Controlled	□ Thoughtful	□ Respectful
□ ______________	□ ______________	□ ______________
□ ______________	□ ______________	□ ______________

STEP 2: CREATE A POWER SPACE. Imagine a space in front of you on the floor. Make it a particular shape or symbol (a circle or square or triangle or something more personal for you) and give it a specific color.

STEP 3: ACCESS A RESOURCE STATE. Pick one of the five resource states you chose and then identify a one-time event in your past when you fully experienced that state. Go back and relive the memory and really connect with the state as you experienced it in that time and place.

STEP 4: ADD THE RESOURCE STATE. Now put that memory into the power space in front of you. See yourself in the memory having that resource state fully and completely. Specifically, watch how you experienced and expressed the resource state in that time and place - body posture, breathing rate, facial expressions, etc.

STEP 5: EXPERIENCE THE POWER. When you are ready, take a step forward into your power space. As you do, step right into your body within the memory and take that resource state on fully and completely. As you relive the experience be aware of what you see, what you hear, your breathing and every sensation you feel in your body.

STEP 6: AMPLIFY THE POWER. At this point, if you have previously added any resource states to your power space bring your awareness of all those back into your mind. As they come to mind notice how it mingles and melds with the resource state you have just added.

Become aware of a totally new power state being created from the combination of all the resource states you have added to your power space up to and including the current one. Really take all these resources on fully and completely, paying special attention to all the small idiosyncrasies and cues which make you aware of how you know you are experiencing this powerful new state of mind.

STEP 7: STEP OUT. After you have really gotten a sense of the power state you have created, take a step backwards out of your power space leaving that state there. Relax your muscles and shake off any residual effects you may feel.

STEP 8: REPEAT. Now, repeat steps 3-7 for each of the resource states you have chosen, using the same power space each time. As you do this, combine the new resource state with all the previous ones you have already put in your power space.

Each time you'll notice a new power state emerging from the combination of all the power states you have added - including the last one. After you've added the final resources state you chose then move on to step 9.

STEP 9: MAKE IT AUTOMATIC. Once again, step into your power space and take on the final power state fully and completely. Pay special attention to all the physiological aspects, both obvious and subtle, that are associated with this new power state.

Step back out and shake off the state. Step forward noticing how quickly and fully you can re-access your power state and take a breath as you say to yourself, "I can do this!" (Or some other mantra of your choosing.)

Repeat this process of stepping out and shaking it off, stepping back into your power state as you take a controlled breath, and say to yourself, "I can do this!" Keep repeating this process until you can take on you power state easily and effortlessly the instant you step forward, take the breath and say your mantra.

The most important aspect of working with your own state of mind is noticing the physiological components that are associated with particular mental and emotional states. By taking the time to develop your awareness of the idiosyncratic cues you associate with the states you use for peak performance you will have greater control over your personal state of mind through the mind-body connection. These cues are the physiological aspects that you can consciously change which will make your mind access a particular resourceful state.

> ***In order to avoid feeling powerless you must have a Power State which you can utilize when dealing with workplace bullies.***

Now, it's valuable here to recognize that some cues may be idiosyncratic - they will be unique to you - while other cues might be shared by many people. Certain types of gestures may vary in meaning from culture to culture while other components of physiological cues are shared between cultures, such as facial expressions.

The problem is that many people tend to assume that behavioral cues for certain states, such as one's breathing patterns, facial expressions, tone of voice, etc. all mean the same thing for everyone. This can really create problems when communicating with other people because incorrect assumptions lead to confusion.

Recognizing that your unconscious mind connects certain idiosyncratic cues to certain mental and emotional states of mind, which may or may not be shared by the people around you, will help avoid misinterpretation of the non-verbal communication from others.

FUNDAMENTAL LESSONS & LEARNINGS...

- A person's state of mind will directly impact how effective they will be in any given situation.
- In order to use verbal self defense to the best of your abilities it's important to have a means for controlling your state.
- You can access and re-access specific states by recalling past events where you experienced the state and reproduce the physiological cues you associate with that state - this utilizes the mind-body connection in order to induce the desired state of mind.
- By combining five (5) resource states it's possible to create a Power State to counteract negative feelings of being bullied. This also helps you be more effective when applying verbal self defense tactics.

MAKING THE RIGHT CONNECTIONS

"Anger is the feeling that makes your mouth work faster than your mind."
Evan Esar

You likely know someone whom you find just rubs you the wrong way. They are not necessarily a bad person, but it seems they just know how to push your buttons. When this happens it can occasionally leave a person so angry or upset they are seeing red and ready for a fight.

As we've already discussed, what they're doing or saying simply goes against your personal values, and that's the reason you respond with a negative feeling. However, there is another way to think of this person's inappropriate behaviors under these circumstances.

The Conditioned Response

When you respond by automatically getting upset due to a person's natural way of being, it's sometimes said to be one of your triggers. More specifically, something the person is doing or saying is what triggers a negative response in you.

In science, this process of connecting an internal response (such as a negative emotion) to a specific external trigger (such as a bullying behavior) is known as Pavlovian Conditioning. Many people recognize this process because it's named after the original, and most famous, example of a classical conditioning experiment done by Ivan Petrovich Pavlov incorporating the salivary conditioning of dogs.

During his research on the physiology of digestion in dogs Pavlov noticed that, rather than simply salivating in the presence of the meat powder they were given, the dogs began to salivate in the presence of the lab technician who normally fed them. From this observation he predicted that, if a particular stimulus in the dog's surroundings were present when the dog was presented with the meat powder, then this stimulus would become associated with food and cause salivation on its own.

> ***Teach your unconscious mind to make the activation of your Power State an automatically triggered response to feelings of being bullied.***

In his initial experiment, Pavlov used a metronome to call the dogs to their food and, after a few repetitions, the dogs started to salivate in response to the metronome. Thus, a neutral stimulus (i.e. the metronome) became a conditioned stimulus (i.e. the trigger) as a result of consistent pairing with the unconditioned stimulus (i.e. the meat powder).

Pavlov referred to this learned relationship as a *Conditional Reflex*. In scientific communities today it's more commonly referred to as *Conditioned Response*. In the field of NLP this formula for stimulus-response conditioning has been expanded to include links between aspects of experience other than purely environmental cues and behavioral responses. This implies that one internal thought is able to trigger another. A simple example is remembering a visual image of a good experience and having it trigger the positive emotional state that originally accompanied it.

Now, in regards to verbal self defense, rather than having a mindless knee-jerk reflex to bullying behaviors it's possible to intentionally connect a chosen state to behaviors which used to simply push your buttons. We can now use Pavlov's strategy to establish an unconscious, automatic mental process which activates your personal power state whenever you would have normally responded with a sense of being bullied. Just like a bully conditions a victim to feel bad, we are going to use the same process as a tool for self empowerment.

RE-CONDITIONING YOUR RESPONSE

In order for a verbal defender to have the ability to access their power state as a way to ensure peak performance capabilities it's necessary to re-program the original conditioning. Be aware that we are not trying to remove or delete anything; rather, we want to merely replace the old conditioning. This is so we can still utilize the original bullying behaviors as a trigger for an emotional state - the only difference is that they will trigger your power state rather than the un-useful response of feeling bullied.

The way to do this is almost identical to the original conditioning which Pavlov used. The only difference is that, during the initial programming stage, you will use internally imagined stimulus rather than an actual external experience.

DEVELOPING YOUR SKILLS & ABILITIES…

TRIGGERING YOUR POWER STATE

The process of training the unconscious part of your mind to use your power state when you want/need it begins with connecting it to those times of conflict. In situations of bullying it's necessary for your mind to avoid being controlled by your emotions while still being able to respond to them. This way you can train yourself to access your power state and stay in control instead of having the feelings of being mentally and emotionally abused override your focus.

In the first part of this exercise you can work with past experiences as a way to show your mind what you want.

Then, in the second part you want to imagine future events so your unconscious mind can get the idea of how you will do it in the future.

STEP 1: ACKNOWLEDGE WHAT WAS. To get yourself started, begin by thinking of a one-time experience in your past where you dealt with someone who treated you in an inappropriate way. It can be something they did, something they said or a combination of both. However it happened, be certain it's an event that you believe you handled poorly and wish you could have been more centered, focused and prepared for.

When you've thought of an experience like this, go back in your memory prior to the start of the event. Once there, pause the experience and imagine moving into an observer position for the event. Pretend you're standing next to the situation and can see the You in the memory and the other person involved.

From this position play the memory and watch the You in the event getting bullied. See how you experienced the situation and watch as you did your best to handle it. As you imagine watching yourself take time to notice how your unbalanced state of mind caused you to be ineffective in dealing with the person.

STEP 2: CHANGE YOUR REACTION. Stop the memory when you get to the end and rewind it back to the beginning. This time, before you start it again, step into the You in the memory.

Now run the event forward slowly, experiencing what you experienced through your own senses. Notice what you see, hear, feel, say, etc. As it progresses, be aware of the first moment you notice a negative feeling. As soon as you catch the initial negative response stop the memory and check to discover what it's a reaction to.

Figure out what it is that you perceive as inappropriate. Specifically, was it the person's words, their tone of voice or perhaps their body language?

As soon as you know what it is, access the Power State you recently created. Take on all the characteristics of that state of mind and get yourself ready to deal with what is coming.

Now… truthfully, you cannot change what was said or what happened. Instead, simply focus on maintaining the power state through the event. Stay in control of what you say and how you say it. Avoid letting yourself have a negative emotional reaction to the bully in the experience.

When you get to the end, take a moment to notice what you learned from the event. Get a sense of what ultimate lesson might be learned from this experience before you let go of the memory and return to being mindful of the present moment.

STEP 3: CREATE A PATTERN. Repeat the entire process of steps 1 and 2 using at least two other past experiences you have had where you were bullied.

STEP 4: TRAIN YOUR REACTION. Once you get a sense of what it could be like staying in control using your power state when facing a bully, it's time to imagine having it when you need it. So now you want to imagine creating a possible future experience where you deal with someone being verbally abusive.

You don't need to know how you're going to handle it and there is no need to know the details of how the event will play out. The main focus will be to imagine someone treating you in a way that, in the past, would have left you feeling bullied.

Create a bullying experience where you have to put up with someone in a situation where the person is either doing or saying something that you believe is hurtful. It can be the way they talk to you, their tone of voice or even their body language. Whatever it is that they do, you want to be aware of the behavior that is unacceptable to you.

The one difference with this *future memory* (as compared to the *past memories* you were working with in steps 1-3) is that you want to experience the event while constantly maintaining your power state and staying centered. The event you make up in your mind can be short and simple so long as it's something you believe could truly happen to you.

Try to avoid imagining that you get the upper hand in any way. Instead, just pretend that you have to put up with the situation as best as you can without letting the other person's words or actions cause you to have any negative emotional reactions - stay in your power state throughout the imagined experience.

STEP 5: MAKE IT YOUR PATTERN. Having pretended to experience a bullying event while holding your center and being in your power state, now do it again with two other made up scenarios. Go through the whole process of step 4 with two other imagined events you make up in your mind.

This process is teaching your unconscious mind to relate your power state to the bullying behaviors of others. Before you have a negative emotional reaction to the mental or emotional abuse of someone you want to have your mind automatically react by having you take on your power state.

FUNDAMENTAL LESSONS & LEARNINGS...

- When you respond by automatically getting upset because of a person's natural way of being, it's referred to as a trigger.
- It is possible to intentionally condition yourself to unconsciously, automatically trigger your power state whenever you would have normally responded with a sense of being bullied.
- One way to create this ability is for us to repeatedly practice triggering a power state using an imagined or remembered mental stimulus rather than an actual external experience.

PART V

USING VERBAL SELF DEFENSE

As verbal defenders we recognize that people are doing the best they can at any given moment in time. We say that everybody makes the best decision possible in the moment (even bullies) because it's the only thing they know to do, based upon everything they've learned up until now.

However, this does not give a bully permission to do whatever they want. It's one thing to say, "I was only doing what I thought was the right thing to do at the time." It's a whole different story to use that as an excuse when you already know that it's going to hurt people. A bully who tries to get away with that is simply unwilling to take responsibility for their choice. Prior to knowing that it hurts someone, the behavior is generated unconsciously and is not technically considered a conscious decision.

With that concept in mind it is only for our own emotional safety that we, as verbal defenders, choose to consider a bully's behavior as the best they are able to do for now. By thinking of it that way we can avoid the natural reaction of taking their words and actions as personal attacks. This is where we can be the better person by taking an attitude which allows us to accept the bully while we work to change their bullying behaviors.

VALIDATION FOR FEELING INVALIDATED

Whenever someone feels slighted they are commonly focused on how they were treated unfairly. This may or may not be the reality of things but it is how they perceived the experience.

In situations like this the person is upset because, unconsciously, they feel that their model of the world has been put into question. This could be directly stated, such as someone telling them, "It's stupid to think that," or it could be implied through actions, such as when someone breaks a rule the person believes about the world, like: "You should not stand inside someone else's personal space." In both examples someone's words or actions are telling the person that their way of thinking and acting is invalid.

Now, we all know that no one likes to be wrong, so the result is that if the person who feels hurt does not argue the point being challenged then they will go away feeling bad. In fact, they not only need to argue the point, they have to prove that what they believe about the world is true; they need their point of view to be validated by the offender.

FOR FURTHER CLARIFICATION…

COMMON DEFENSIVE TACTICS

In order to get personal validation, someone who feels slighted usually becomes defensive and starts to try and explain themselves. The process for doing this can include any number of tactics such as:

- Trying to justify one's own point of view based upon their past personal experiences.
- Reasoning with the other person to get one's own point of view to fit within their mental map.
- Attempting to compromise and find middle ground between different points of view.
- Rationalization of the different points of view and perceptions in order to confirm the validity of one's own opinion(s).
- Discounting of the other person's opinions and perceptions - basically speaking, *invalidating their mental map of the world.*
- Simply ignoring information and perceptions from the other people's point of view.

As a person argues in defense of their own model of the world, they have a tendency to try and explain themselves while attempting to remain sympathetic to the other person's needs. The problem is, as we learned earlier, when you try to lump together your own point of view with someone else's it can create confusion in what you are trying to communicate.

Accept a bully as a person while you work toward finding a way to convince them to change their use of abusive words and behaviors.

The 6 step verbal self defense model incorporates all the important and useful components of normal human defensive tactics in a way that is simple to remember and easy to do. Although it may not always get you everything you want in life, this model will provide you with a structure to help you be clear in your communication while also providing you with the feedback necessary to identify when it's time to try a new tactic. Often people do not know how to determine the point when they need to give up on what they are currently doing and try doing something different.

A Fluid 3 Point Base

"With every gust of wind,
the butterfly changes its place on the willow."
Matsuo Basho

Since we, as verbal defenders, know that a person's behaviors are not who they are, it's easier to accept the person and simply focus on changing their behavior. This makes it more acceptable to others because it still validates their model of the world while focusing on finding more appropriate alternatives.

With this in mind, there are three components which must be clearly defined before anyone can effectively use verbal self defense. Those three components are comprised of:

1) Awareness
2) Intention
3) Focus

These components allow us to effectively prepare ahead of time for the issues which come up when using verbal self defense. The first concern above all else is that we are required to know what it is that we want. In order to effectively shift a bully's behavior we need to know what option we want them to change to.

> ***Awareness, Intention and Focus are the Key Elements to effective Verbal Self Defense.***

So, by first being Aware of what words and behaviors are upsetting us we can decide what alternative, appropriate form of communication we want from the person. It's that specific way of interacting that we want the other person to use which is our Intended Outcome. Then it becomes a matter of Focusing on finding a way to effectively communicate that intention to the other person without them knocking us off balance or taking control of the conversation.

FOR FURTHER CLARIFICATION…

CREATING YOUR FOUNDATION

AWARENESS. Using your *awareness* is all about taking the time to be mindful of negative emotions and identify what specific behavior(s) a person is doing, or what they're saying, which create those negative emotions in you. In some situations it's possible to become aware of more than one potential problem, such as someone yelling, using profanity, calling you names and/or acting physically intimidating.

In a case like that you need to determine the behavior which causes you the greatest amount of concern; which one is the greatest threat to your mental and emotional safety? That's the bullying tactic you want to use your verbal self defense to deal with first.

Always remember that it's important to utilize your skills to handle only one threat at a time. This helps to avoid being overwhelmed and decreases the potential of getting sidetracked.

INTENTION. Setting an *intention* is the point in the process where you determine what you want the person to do differently in order to relieve your negative emotional reaction. This should be described in sensory specific detail such as what you will see the person do or hear the person say differently. Your explanation should be as clear, specific and direct as possible in order to minimize any confusion or misinterpretation. Some examples could be to "speak in a quieter tone of voice," "refrain from swearing," "only refer to me by my name" or "step out of my personal space."

If possible, it's useful to have more than one option for the person to do for each bullying behavior you want them to change. This will increase the chance of that person finding an acceptable choice which works within their own mental map of the world.

FOCUS. In order to get what you want it's necessary to stay *focused* on going after the intention you have set. This requires you to politely avoid entangling yourself in any other issue or concern that does not pose an even greater threat than the one being dealt with.

To do this you must start by maintaining a constant mental focus on directing the conversation towards addressing the issue which was determined in the first step of awareness to be the biggest concern. This means a good verbal defender is prepared for the bully to try and re-direct the topic towards his/her own desired outcome.

When this happens you need to have a standard phrase or come-back that puts the attention back to the issue you want to deal with. Some examples include things like:

- "I realize that what you're talking about is important, but before we can discuss that I need you to agree to..."
- "You are absolutely right and it's important for us to work out the detail of how to deal with that, however, before I can go any further on this I need you to agree to..."
- "That is a valid point and I'll be happy to talk about that further, once you agree to..."

- "You have a right to feel that way and we definitely need to find a solution for you, and in order to do that I first need you to agree to…"

After you make the re-direct statement above you can complete the sentence with the intention you set as the desired outcome.

Once you have gone through the process of building your 3 point foundation it's necessary to maintain it. As you know, your senses never shut off. This means that your awareness is constantly feeding new information to your brain. As this is happening it turns into an ongoing process of cycling through the steps of Awareness, Intention and Focus.

In each successive moment you are checking your awareness to see if the original bullying tactic determined to be the biggest concern has been resolved. In comparison, you're also checking at the same time to determine if there are any new and more dangerous concerns. In this way, if something even more abusive happens you can be flexible and easily shift your focus to deal with that instead.

IMAGINE…

Occasionally, customer service agents must deal with clients who feel they have received inadequate service. Most businesses have policies and procedures for handling these types of complaints which customer service representatives must follow. In highly stressful times it's easy for things to escalate quickly if those company policies do not immediately get the customer the solution they have asked for.

One good example of businesses that are inundated with these kinds of situations is Veterinarian Clinics. At a vet clinic the people in charge are responsible for the care of client's pet. When circumstances do not work out well the pet's owner can become distraught and easily upset. Combined with the fact that reception staff members do not necessarily have enough information to always answer all their questions, nor the authority to overturn company policies, this can easily lead to an unsatisfactory outcome for the client.

As an example, if a pet owner becomes verbally abusive regarding the bill for the services provided to their pet the office staff can utilize verbal self defense to deal with them. However, as they try to deal with the client's abusive language the customer might become even more aggressive in an attempt to intimidate the staff into giving him what he wants. In this case let's pretend that he starts banging his fist on the counter.

At that point the staff might feel this new behavior is more concerning than the verbal abuse. This is when they can easily set a new intention to deal with it and, starting at step 1, use verbal self defense to address the problem. Once the issue of the client's physical aggression has been resolved then staff can easily go back to the step on the verbal self defense model where they left off in regard to the customer's verbal abuse.

After the greatest threat has been resolved you can re-check your awareness to see if there are any other concerns which need to be addressed. This cycle goes on until all bullying tactics have been cleared up. When you reach that point then you can communicate with the person in a respectable, professional and civilized manner.

FUNDAMENTAL LESSONS & LEARNINGS...

- First, use your Awareness to determine what bullying behavior is upsetting you.
- Then, decide what alternative, appropriate form of communication you want the bully to use instead and set your Intention on achieving that outcome
- Finally, Focus on effectively communicating your desired intention to the other person without allowing them to knock you off balance or take control of the conversation.
- Always keep your awareness open to other events which could potentially be more harmful, and be flexible in shifting your focus to anything you determine to be a greater concern.

THE 6 STEPS OF VERBAL SELF DEFENSE

"The only real defense is active defense."
Mao Zedong

Once you have set your intention and begun focusing on it you need a simple set of guidelines to ensure you are communicating as effectively as possible. Even though you have skills to stay mentally and emotionally balanced it's still useful to have a predetermined set of steps which will cover all the components necessary to maximize your chance of success - in this case, to convince a bully to change their behavior

This is where the verbal self defense 6 step model comes in. In this model for verbal defensive tactics everything is divided into steps in order to respect and utilize both the attacker's and the defender's mental map of the world.

The six steps happen in the following order:

1) **Acknowledge your attacker.**
2) **Ask for your intention.**
    - If you do not get agreement go to the next step.
3) **Justify the request from your perspective.**
    - If you do not get agreement go to the next step.
4) **Reason with your attacker's perspective.**
    - If you do not get agreement go to the next step.
5) **Confirm their unwillingness to change.**
    - If you do not get agreement go to the next step.
6) **Actively pursue an alternative solution.**

These six steps provide you with a multitude of benefits when dealing with workplace bullies:

- It allows you to acknowledge the situation and what is happening without anyone taking it personally;
- Using this process gives your attacker the benefit of the doubt regarding hurtful intentions by providing them with the opportunity to deal with the situation in a mature, professional manner;
- You actually give your attacker not just one, but rather, four chances to adjust their abusive communication tactics and be more reasonable;
- During the process of going through the model you get a clear opportunity to explain things from your own point of view;
- As a demonstration of your own value for effective communication there is a step that recognizes the whole thing from the attacker's point of view;
- This model also allows you to show flexibility in finding an agreeable solution to the situation; and
- Finally, this process gives you a clear means of realizing when your current course of action is never going to be successful. This way you can change tactics and avoid wasting any further time and energy.

STEP 1: ACKNOWLEDGE WHAT IS HAPPENING

There are people in this world who are more the type of person to talk *at* you rather than talk *with* you. Many of you have probably experienced someone like this somewhere in your past. The main concern with bullies who communicate in this way is that any verbal self defense you use will not be effective because they are not actually treating the situation as a two-way conversation.

So, the first step in verbal self defense is to engage a bully by *Acknowledging* their words and behaviors. This will give the person a sense of being listened to which increases the likelihood of them being more open to listening in return.

When a person is communicating with someone, that person wants to know that they are getting their message across to whomever they are communicating with. For them to feel that they are being effective at communicating their message they require some way of recognizing this.

Bullies are usually looking for non-verbal cues to know that they are being effective at controlling the other person. Since a good verbal defender remains in control of their mental state using a power state, the bully needs that feedback in another form. So, to ensure that we remain in complete control, it's more useful to do this with our words instead.

To acknowledge someone with words it's best to begin with phrases such as, "I recognize…," "I notice…," "I respect…," "I appreciate…," or "I agree..."

After that you can point out some kind of sensory specific awareness you have such as, "…by the way you are leaning over me…," "…by the way you are speaking in such a harsh tone of voice…," or "…by the way you are banging your fist on the table..."

This is the point where, if you choose to, you can point out the importance of the situation. An example of this would be, "…it's important for us to talk about this…," "…it seems you feel this is quite an important point…," "… that this is something we definitely need to resolve…"

This is a simple way to acknowledge what is happening within the interaction between you and the bully, without belittling or discounting them. The first step of Acknowledgment should be immediately followed up with step 2.

STEP 2: ASK FOR YOUR INTENTION

During the initial encounter with a person there was a point where you became aware that you were feeling something negative because you were being bullied. That first awareness of negative feelings is what triggers your power state and allowed you to recognize what abusive behavior the bully was doing that created an unpleasant reaction within you.

After that you set an intention as to what you want them to do in place of that abusive behavior. This is the step in verbal self defense where you first *Ask* for what you want. To do that you must remember that it's important to give instruction in sensory specific details. That means, you tell the bully exactly what you want from them.

> ***Make sure you build whatever mental states you need into your Power State so that you will be able to ask directly for what you want.***

An example might be if their using a posture of intimidation you can ask them to "...please take step back." If they are yelling then you could ask them to "...please lower the volume of your voice." Perhaps if they are banging their hands on the desk then you could ask that they "...please keep your hands back from my desk."

Notice that these are all direct requests. When using verbal self defense it's necessary to avoid implying, suggesting or hinting at what you want. Statements that are not useful for verbal self defense are things like, "...I'd appreciate it if you could take a step back," "...most people around here prefer to discuss things in a quieter voice than that," "...it is considered inappropriate to bang your hand on the desk like that."

None of those are asking for anything - they are all just statements of fact. The bully may choose to believe your comments do not apply to them; otherwise, they probably would have been behaving that way to begin with.

Another point to take note of is that nowhere in steps 1 or 2 do you attempt to explain yourself or get them to understand why you want the intention you ask for. Instead, you simply acknowledge the situation and politely ask them to adjust their behavior. No blame, no judgment and no power struggle.

If you get what you have asked for then everything is clearly taken care of. However, if you do not get positive results after step 1 and 2 then it's necessary to move on to step 3.

Step 3: Justify it From Your Point of View

Many people in this world find it a natural reaction to want to explain why they want something at the time they ask for it. It's a form of trying to justify why one's request is acceptable. Since this is common for many of us it's step 3 on the verbal self defense model.

The main concern here is to remain true to your own point of view. Often, when trying to justify ourselves we pretend to figure out what we think the other person needs to hear in order to convince them that our belief about what we want is right. When this happens it risks the confusion of our point of view with their point of view.

So, when justifying your intention in verbal self defense avoid taking on the other person's point of view. Stay completely in your own mental map of the world and explain it from your perception. Describe what you think is happening and what that means to you. Then explain what personal value your desired intention has for you before you ask for it again.

In the process of doing this step you might say things like, "Please understand that, to me, it's important that people respect my personal space by not leaning over me when they are talking to me. So, can you please take a step back?" or, "In the office I think it's a professional courtesy to refrain from raising your voice and disturbing one's co-workers. Can you please lower the volume of your voice?" or, "I must tell you that when you bang your fist on my desk like that it feels a bit like you're threatening me. I need to ask: can you please keep your hands off my desk while we talk?"

When attempting to justify why you want them to do what you asked it's helpful to explain why it's important to you and how you think it's valuable to the interaction between the two of you right now. After you have justified your request, remember to ask for it again using the same format as you did in step 2. If you do not get the result you want then move on to step 4.

STEP 4: REASON FROM THEIR POINT OF VIEW

Since many of us are taught to always consider things from other people's point of view it's going to be one of our automatic responses. To properly utilize this ability it deserves its own step on the verbal self defense model.

Remember that when you are doing this it's important to keep your own opinions, perceptions, beliefs and values out of any interpretation you make of the other person's communication. When considering the other person's point of view look specifically for what they are actually trying to accomplish in communicating with you.

Whatever it is that they are intending to accomplish by communicating with you this way, you want to connect it to your intention. You can do this by simply referring to whatever they are focusing on and declaring, before any progress can be made toward their desired outcome, they will need to agree to what you are asking for.

The easiest way would be to simply state it like, "I realize you want to talk about me staying late, however, before I am willing to do that I need you to take a step back. Will you please take a step back?" or' "I get the obvious sense that because you are yelling this must be a very intense topic for you, however, before I am willing to talk any further about this I'd like you to lower the volume of your voice. Will you please lower the volume of your voice?" or' "Whether or not you think that banging your fist on my desk is going to make me more agreeable to your request, I am not willing to talk about this further unless you agree to keep your hands off my desk. Will you please keep your hands away from my desk while we discuss this?"

Notice in each case that the possible desired goal of the bully - as determined by non-judgmentally considering the interaction from their point of view - is first connected to the intention of the verbal defender. Then, it's immediately followed by asking for that intention.

This is necessary so that if you are ever required to justify your course of action, you can clearly and honestly say, "I specifically asked them at each step…" This avoids any possible argument that you were not clear in communicating your expectations to your attacker.

So, for this step, consider the other person's position in this interaction. What is it they are doing and how do they perceive their communication? Think about what they could be attempting to accomplish by speaking to you in this way or acting in this manner. Now, give them a reason why it's valuable for them to do what you have requested by connecting the gain they receive from doing what you ask to their goal in this situation.

Contrary to rewarding a bully for agreeing to your request, an additional tactic is to identify any possible consequences. However, if you are intending to use any kind of threats of consequences during this process, be absolutely certain you can back them up. Never make empty threats or bluff in verbal self defense. If necessary, make your alternate course of action vague or ambiguous. You might not be able to guarantee that you can get them terminated, but you can warn them that: "If you do not change your abusive behavior, I intend to file a complaint."

Overall, the goal of this step on the verbal self defense model is that you want to give your attacker a reason why it is valuable for them to do what you have requested by connecting the benefit they receive from doing what you ask to their desired outcome in the situation. Alternatively, you can also confirm any consequences which they need to be aware of if they do NOT agree to what you're asking. (Or, if you choose to, you can explain both.)

After you've given them reason to agree to your intention always remember to ask again for what you want just like you did in step 2. If they do not agree to what you have asked for then it's time to move on to step 5.

Step 5: Confirm There Is an Impasse

A good verbal defender has flexibility in how they communicate and in the way they will allow the bully to change their abusive behavior; however, some bullies are not as accommodating. In this world there are going to be people who are unwilling to accept responsibility for how their words and actions impact the people around them. In these cases you may not be able to get simple and effective change from your abuser, however, you always want to make sure you tried everything possible to find a solution before you take any alternate form of action.

To do this, a good verbal defender will simply ask if there is any way that the person would be willing to find an agreeable solution to the problem behavior. It's important to remember that by the time you get to this step on the verbal self defense model you have already; acknowledged the problem; asked for what you want; explained yourself and asked for what you want a second time; tried to get them to understand the benefit from their point of view and then you even asked them a third time.

After completing each step, always remember to clearly ask again for what you want - exactly as you did in Step 2.

It's then fair to say that, by this point, you've tried every reasonable means of finding a solution to the conflict that any average person could be expected to do. Anyone who says otherwise will usually say that the proper thing to do is just, "Learn to put up with it," - *which is absolutely wrong!* That is what created the bully in the first place - when no one confronts the bully, they learn that it's okay to treat people inappropriately and without dignity. It goes so far as to give the public impression that all the people in the organization are likely to be unprofessional and disrespectful.

So, now it's time to draw the proverbial line in the sand. This is the last chance you will give the bully to change before you accept the impasse and move to an alternate line of action. Now, when you do this step it will be a simple, one-sentence request for confirmation of whether or not the bully is unwilling to help resolve the issue.

When asking for this confirmation for whether or not they are refusing to do what you want, the question you will use is:

> *"Is there anything I can say or do right now that will allow you to choose to [FILL IN THE INTENTION YOU ASKED FOR IN STEP 2]?"*

Then, (in order to be completely clear) follow this question by asking one last time for them to do what you have been requesting in each previous step. The purpose behind this is that when you ask the confirmation question it's exactly that - a request for confirmation. It's not a request for them to change their abusive words or behavior. This is the reason why you follow up your request for confirmation by asking them to do what you want in a sentence of its own.

The very next thing they do should be taken as the answer to your question - either they agree to do as you have asked and they do it, or they don't do it and that means they don't agree. This step in the model is Yes or No. So long as they are willing to do what you have asked the answer is confirmed as yes; otherwise you will consider the answer to be no.

Even if they just try to negotiate further with you it means No at this point. You have attempted to be flexible and work with them for the last 3 steps in the model so any attempt on their part now is just tactics for stalling until they can find another way to avoid accepting your request. If the result of asking for confirmation does not lead to an unequivocal agreement in your mind then you will move on to step 6 of the verbal self defense model.

In the same sense, if they make a request for something that is absolutely outside what is acceptable to you, then the answer is equivalent to No. Absurd, unethical or inappropriate replies to your confirmation question are typically meant to be condescending in nature. No matter what their intention is in giving you such an answer, your reply can quite simply be, "Well… it looks like we just aren't going to be able to come to an agreement here." From there you simply go to step 6.

STEP 6: TAKE ACTION TO FIND AN ALTERNATE SOLUTION

Now it's time to change tactics and do something different to get the bully to change how they are treating you. If possible, have a plan prior to reaching this step. Know what your next course of action is if you don't get your attacker to shift their mentally and emotionally abusive words and actions to something more appropriate.

Often it's beneficial to know this going into step 4 so that if you attempt to use any threat of consequence then you're staying true to your word. This is important to a verbal defender because it sets a kind of precedence for the bully in the future. Remember that bullying is usually not an isolated event; it's just the way the person is, so you can likely expect them to do something abusive again in the future. When that time comes you want the person to know that when you warn them of the consequences, you will follow through with your intentions.

In the same way that you never bluff, you should never back down. It's common for abusers to abruptly repent and make promises to change their ways at this point in the conflict. The moment that there appears to be actual consequence for their actions, bullies suddenly want to quickly avoid that by trying to get you to not follow through with your threat. Now they want you to agree to give them another chance, and they will even have excuses like, "I didn't realize this was so important to you."

No matter what they say, never back down. Now is the time to follow through. If you don't, then all you will have accomplished by going through this whole process is to teach them exactly how far they can push you and how much you will put up with. You will have effectively given them an actual sentence they can listen for to know when they finally need to insincerely agree to your request. If you back off now, from this point forward whenever they hear you make your confirmation statement in step 5 they will know they need to pretend to give in for awhile in order to keep you playing their game.

> ***In verbal self defense you should never bluff and never back down. If you reach Step 6, always go through with your alternate choice of action.***

By doing exactly as you have said you would do it shows absolute commitment on your part and the other person will very quickly identify that you mean business. You drew a line in the sand and they crossed it, and now it's time for you to try a new tactic.

I've heard people say, "Every ending is a new beginning." The same is true with verbal self defense. The final step in the verbal self defense model for one opponent is sometimes the first step in the model for another opponent. An example is going and speaking to their supervisor or filing a complaint with the company's Human Resource Department. In both of these situations you can use the same process of verbal self defense to try and get them to help you fix the problem. You are now fully aware that you need to try something different; you've given the message that you intend to take the next step; and you can now focus on following through on it.

When you go to the bully's Supervisor or a Human Resource Coordinator acknowledge what has happened so far, and explain all the things you've done to try and solve the issue. Then ask for what you want them to do about it. If it does not get the results you want, follow it up by justifying your position and ask them again. If that does not work, make them aware of the pros and cons for them (reason) to assist you in getting the bully to stop the abusive behaviors. If it still does not work, confirm the impasse and then be prepared to try something else. At that point it might be something like *taking legal action* or *finding a new job*.

In whatever way you choose to handle this step it's important to be aware that this is the point in the conflict when you can know with certainty that your current course of action will *not* get the results you want. It may seem tough to admit because most people want to believe that they can find a solution, and you are right in thinking there is a solution; but the way you are trying to achieve it is not working.

Einstein defined *insanity* as: "Doing the same thing over and over expecting a different result;" however, I personally interpret that as: "If you keep doing what has not previously worked over and over again you can expect to go insane."

FOR FURTHER CLARIFICATION…

PERSONALIZE THE PROCESS

At every stage of the verbal self defense model it's necessary for you to remember that it's your choice how you phrase/communicate what you need to. You have to choose how you personally would prefer to handle things at each step.

The goal of utilizing this model for verbal self defense is to give you guidance around what to focus on and what you need to communicate, but it's completely up to you how you phrase it. In whatever way you express yourself it's important to do so in a way that adheres to your own personal beliefs and values.

With the same regard, your communication style must

fit within the group mentality of the office. Along with your own personal beliefs and values about what you think the right thing is to do and say when defending yourself, also consider how others will perceive your communication. There is little point in overcoming minor bullying in a way that will cause even worse problems for you in other ways.

If possible, it can be much more effective to utilize the standards and expectations of the group on how to deal with the bullying behavior - so if the company has policies and procedures in place for dealing with workplace bullying, start with those and attempt to work the verbal self defense model within those guidelines.

FUNDAMENTAL LESSONS & LEARNINGS...

- The 6 steps of the verbal self defense model are: 1) Acknowledge, 2) Ask, 3) Justify, 4) Reason, 5) Confirm, and 6) Act.
- Acknowledging the person gives them a sense of being listened to, which increases the likelihood of them being more open to listening to you in return.
- When you ask for what you want, remember that it's important to give instructions as sensory specific behaviors - *what will you see the person do, hear them say, etc.*
- In justifying your intention explain what personal value your desired intention has for you before you ask for it again.
- To reason with the person, make reference to whatever they are focusing on and tell them that, before any progress can be made toward their desired outcome, you will need them to agree to what you are asking for. Then ask for it again.
- To confirm that there is no immediate solution to the conflict, ask them, "Is there anything I can say or do right now that will allow you to choose to [FILL IN THE INTENTION YOU ASKED FOR IN STEP 2]?" Then, ask one last time for them to do what you have been requesting in each previous step.

- If your confirmation is not successful in getting the person to agree to change their bullying behaviors, then it's time to take action and try a different tactic.
- *Never bluff* and *never back down* - if you get to step 6 always go forward with any consequences you have committed to, otherwise you only teach the bully exactly how they can control you.

STEPPING UP IN THE REAL WORLD

"War is the spectacular and bloody projection of our everyday living."
Jiddu Krishnamurti

Taking the time now to recall that the person with the most flexibility controls the conversation, it's necessary to look at the ways verbal self defense allows you to increase your own options. In the process of doing this it's of utmost importance to always be using your own personal values and beliefs to make the choices that are right for you. Only by doing it this way will it be possible for you to feel both confident and comfortable with how, when and where you apply the steps of the verbal self defense model in your life.

A Time and Place of Your Choosing

If a workplace bully catches you off guard and attempts to knock you off balance it can often be a simple matter of utilizing your power state to simply get through the experience. The truth is, real life situations of bullying or abuse do not usually present themselves in a way that is conducive to easy and effective verbal self defense. In a lot of cases it may only be afterwards when you actually realize that you need to, and want to, do something to address your concerns.

As a verbal defender it must first and foremost be up to you when and where you take a stand. So, whatever the situation, it's useful to have a means to re-access their mind's representation of the event so you can apply your verbal self defense skills at a time of your choosing. In order to have this freedom to work outside the actual abusive experience when it happens it's necessary to know how to get the bully to remember the original event when you're ready.

The best way to do this is through the simple act of verbally reviewing the step-by-step experiences of the event in detail. This will remind the bully of the original event by taking them through the past experience in their mind as if it were happening in the present.

In doing this it's critical that you use only sensory specific descriptions of exactly what happened from the observer point of view without any labels or interpretations. Go back through the abusive situation sequentially telling the person what actually happened. This will make them play the memory of your explanation in their mind. When this is happening it's much like listening to a story or watching a television show - the person must imagine themselves in the event as you explain it and, in doing so, it will access the actual memory in their mental map.

So, to do this properly and effectively it's necessary to turn on your own memory during the real event as it's actually happening. Whenever you experience feelings of being bullied, be certain to take note of exactly what happens, what is said, what tones of voice are used, body language, etc. That way you will be able to vividly recall all the details of what happened when you are reiterating the original experience to the bully at a later point in time.

Having the ability to re-create the experience and deal with it at a later time and place allows you to better prepare yourself beforehand and figure out what you want to say. This way you can get everything clear in your mind before you have to even begin the process of defending yourself. Once you have reminded the person of the specific situation of bullying that you want to address, then it's a simple process to moving right into the first step of the verbal self defense model.

Pacing Yourself

Another option you have when applying the verbal self defense model is how quickly you progress through the 6 steps. You can always choose to work through the steps of the model at a pace which you are most comfortable with. In the same way, you can combine steps of the model when the urgency of a situation necessitates a more timely resolution.

> ***Always go through the steps of the verbal self defense model in order - that way you can always re-cover your accountability.***

Depending upon the relationship you have with the bully in question, you might choose to consider each step of the verbal self defense model a discussion by itself. In this way you can go through step 1 and 2 with the person one day and then give some time to see if it changes how they communicate with you. Remember that workplace bullying is almost never an isolated event. If you know that a bully will repeat an abusive behavior then you can allow them time to make any necessary adjustments between steps.

You can choose to apply steps 1 and 2, and then wait a few days to see if the person says or does the same inappropriate behavior again. In the event that it happens again you can then apply step 3, and then give them a few days to create some new, appropriate choices of how to interact with you. Should it happen again, you can apply step 4 and see if that works. After that, if they still do not change their abusive behavior then you can choose to proceed to step 5, knowing that the next time it happens after that you will find an alternate means of dealing with the problem.

Instead of giving them time between steps to incorporate the intention you asked for, it's possible to apply the verbal self defense model all in one discussion. If what you desire from the person is agreement to treat you differently, and they are unwilling to listen, then you may choose to proceed to the next step each time you do not get their immediate agreement. In this way you can start by doing step 1 and 2, then wait for an answer. If they do not acknowledge right then and there that they will do as you have asked, then you simply go right into step 3. If you do not get a positive response after step 3, then go to step 4. Should they once again refuse to agree, by doing step 5 right away you can quickly discover if you're going to need to take a different approach.

Those two ways of applying the model are like two ends of the spectrum with a multitude of choices in between; you may choose to do the first couple steps and give the person some time to change; then you might combine the remaining steps all in one follow-up conversation. Alternately, you might combine the first 3 all in one discussion and do the other steps each in their own separate conversation. Perhaps you might choose to just combine steps 3 and 4, or some other combination in your own way.

Whatever way you decide to apply the verbal self defense model you should always go through all the steps in order. The main reason for this is to ensure you cover your accountability - if you're ever pressed to explain yourself and how you handled the problem, you'll be able to more easily and effortlessly recount exactly what you did and the summary of what you said for each step of the model.

FOR FURTHER CLARIFICATION...

DEALING WITH EXTREMES

In situations of extreme concern, such as a case of sexual harassment, you may even decide to do the whole model all in one continuous speech. Should you ever feel threatened in a way which would require you to physically defend yourself it's useful to use the verbal self defense model as a preemptive warning about your concerns - make sure you Cover Your Accountability *(C.Y.A.)*

To do this you can simply go through each step of the model saying exactly what you need to say and asking for what you want without allowing your attacker time to respond in between your comments. If necessary you may even choose to talk over them if they try to speak. In whatever way you choose to do it, the main goal is to get through the entire model before things escalate to a point where you may need to physically defend yourself.

By using verbal self defense in this way it allows you to confirm to authorities that you tried everything you could to resolve the issue verbally before things got out of hand. As well, by ensuring that your attacker knows that step 6 in your mind is the necessity for physical self defense then you are able to sincerely and confidently say that you clearly warned the person.

The Decreasing Choice of Conflict Escalation

It's true that a core component of being a good verbal defender is flexibility in the way you engage your attacker. In real life, however, it's necessary to take account of how flexible you really want to be.

You learned that your negative emotions are spotlights on boundary violations which are in conflict with your personal values. In the same sense, the intensity of your negative emotion is directly related to the level of importance you put on the particular value being violated.

Now, knowing that everyone has their own mental map of the world, each person will have different values and beliefs. This means other people are allowed to have their own opinions and ways of doing things, but not at the cost of causing you pain and suffering. Acknowledging your right to mental and emotional safety will help set the limits on what you are and are not willing to accept. Thus, what you believe is important about yourself and how you think the world should be/work will be your guidelines on why you use your verbal self defense skills.

Furthermore, the verbal self defense model will set certain restrictions, as well. When you begin the process of verbally defending yourself from a bully you have a very large degree of choice in how you interact and work with the person. As you begin to assert your boundaries and rights to be treated appropriately the other person will likely consider your point of view as an attack on their own mental map of the world. The result will be a continuous escalation in the level of conflict between the two of you.

In direct relation to the escalating level of conflict during the process of applying verbal self defense, your own degree of choice will decrease. With each step you take upwards on the verbal self defense model you will be bringing new opinions and perspectives into the discussion. In order to maintain control and focus during the interaction it's necessary to stay consistent in what information you utilize throughout all 6 steps.

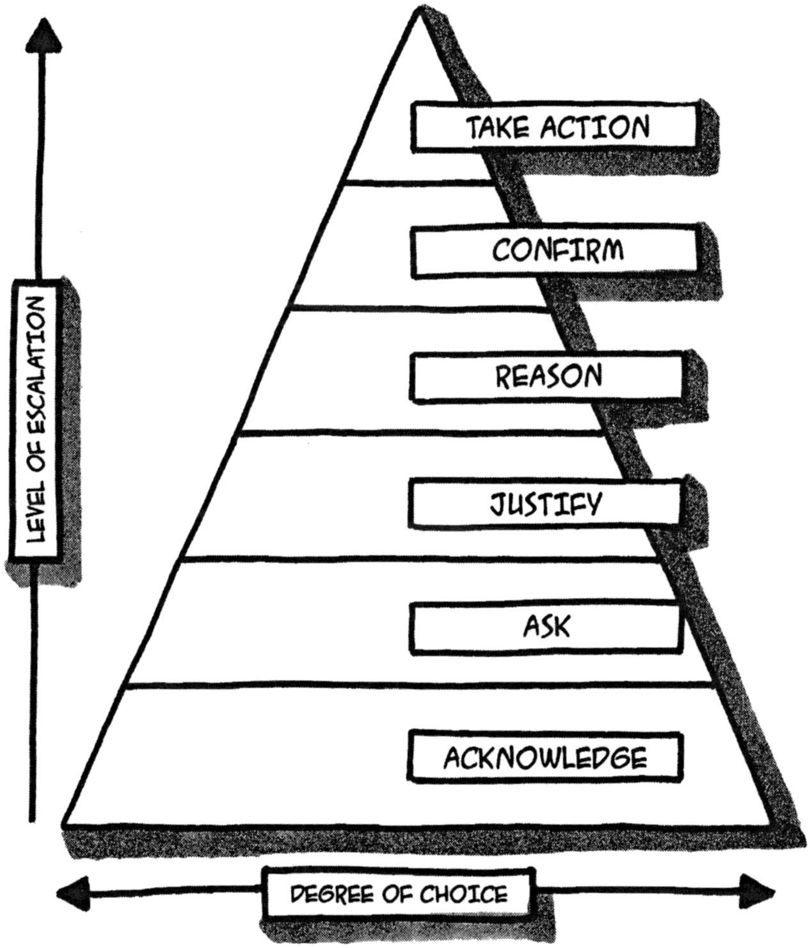

If you ask for a particular intention at step 2 then that'll be the same all the way to the top. If, for some reason you become aware that your intention is *not* achievable, you need to go back to step 1 if you want to ask for a different intention.

As well, remember that when using verbal self defense it's of the utmost importance you never bluff. If you do say something which you are not able or willing to follow through with, then you have the right to acknowledge your error in judgment and correct yourself.

For further clarification...

To Err is Human... Deal With It

Although it's better to use your power state to stay balanced and in control, and to think things through before you say something, people will make mistakes. An example might be when someone (who is extremely angry in the moment) suddenly threatens to contact their lawyer and sue. If the truth of the situation is that the person is not actually going to do that, then they should correct themselves immediately, before the discussion goes any further.

Similarly if, for doing what you ask, you offer a person something that you are not willing or able to get/do, then you should clarify the error right away. Telling someone you will help them with a project that you know you don't have the time for is equivalent to a lie - which is the basis of manipulation, not verbal self defense. Although the mistake may be unintentional, it's still promising a false reward just to get what you want. Acknowledging your error and immediately changing it avoids the risk of causing another confrontation later on.

In some cases bullies will resist as long as possible, expecting to recant and give in when they absolutely have no other option. Usually a person who does this is very good at persuading someone to give them one more chance. Even then, it's common for the person to soon go back to the old patterns of being a bully.

During these instances a verbal defender will usually get all the way to step 6 before the bully suddenly changes and promises to do as they have been asked. In this situation it's still important that you never bluff. If you get to step 5 and request confirmation followed by asking for what you want, and then the person does the bullying behavior again, you need to follow through with taking the next step.

If you have let the bully know at step 4 that you will take the complaint to their supervisor and you reach step 6, then that's what you need to do. A manipulative bully will, at that point, suddenly agree to give you what you ask for while you were using your verbal self defense. In fact, it's something they will usually wait to do until you actually make movement towards following through on your threat - at that moment they know that they will have to do something to placate you for awhile.

You must follow through with the consequences you defined in step 4. Depending on the alternate tactic you planned on using at step 6, you may find it difficult, but it's absolutely necessary that you stay consistent. By pressing ahead with your previously chosen action it sets a precedent that people around you soon realize: "You are absolutely dedicated to doing what's necessary to stop bullying behaviors." Office bullies will only need to experience consequences from bullying you a few times before they quickly learn to simply leave you alone.

The Freedom of Alternative Tactics

In the event you reach step 6 on the verbal self defense model, your degree of choice for handling the situation returns to being infinite. In the same way you had unlimited options to deal with the bully prior to step 1 in your original attempt, once more you can feel free to choose any alternative tactic you think might be effective for handling the issue.

The difference at this point is in regard to what the issue is that you will focus on. During the first attempt at using verbal self defense to change the abusive behavior of the bully you may have identified certain consequences at step 4. If you threatened to take any specific course of action, then that becomes your new intention that you will focus on. In order to take that action as an alternate way to overcome the person's bullying behavior you can utilize the verbal self defense model again.

In the same sense, if you didn't mention any consequence at step 4, or it was really ambiguous (such as, "I'll be unwilling to continue this discussion."), then you can repeat the model with the same person but using a different intention. An example of this is to first use the verbal self defense model to attempt to get someone to, "Refrain from using profanity during your conversation." If you don't achieve that, then the next intention for that same bully might be simply to have him/her leave your office.

IMAGINE...

Imagine a situation where a customer service manager is dealing with a client returning a previously purchased item, and the customer becomes verbally abusive - yelling and calling staff-members derogatory names. If company policies and procedures are not in place to deal with this kind of problem it then becomes the responsibility of the manager to deal with the situation as best as he/she can.

To simplify it, we can use two escalating options of refusing to continue the conversation followed by the choice of having the person removed from the premises. Going through the verbal self defense model with the customer the manager might get to the top and, after having warned the customer at step 4, the manager could simply turn and walk away, refusing to continue the conversation.

At that point, if the customer attempts to follow the manager or tries to escalate the situation, then the manager can go through the verbal self defense model again. This time however, the manager can set the intention of having the customer leave the store, along with the consequence of calling store security if they don't comply. During this second interaction, if the manager reaches the top of the model once more, they can then simply follow through with calling security to have the customer removed from the premises.

> ***Stay open to alternate options to overcome the bullying behavior. That way, if your first attempt does not work, you can easily repeat the model with an alternate choice.***

By keeping your awareness open to searching for different tactics to overcome the issue, you can cycle through the model with each new alternate approach you find in order to deal with the bully and their bullying behaviors. Whatever options you come up with along the way, the end step does not need to be some extreme act of self defense.

The first option you offer a bully may or may not have consequences; however, if that does not convince them to adjust their behavior then you can simply move onto a new option with different consequences. If you so choose, you can decide that each unsuccessful attempt will lead to a worse and worse resulting outcome - the important thing to consider is, "Will this achieve the desired goal of having the bully change their bullying behavior?"

One possible example of a situation where this might happen is dealing with abusive subordinates. One might send an employee home for the day if verbal self defense is unsuccessful the first time, compared with a week suspension the second time, compared to terminating employment in a worst case scenario. In this way the verbal self defense model can simply be repeated for each escalating consequence.

Knowing this possible cycle of increasing consequences ahead of time is often useful, thus it's a good idea to write out a clear outline of ideas for what to do if someone is noncompliant with your request. This way you know exactly what is coming and are better prepared to stay focused on the intention during the discussion rather than trying to determine any possible consequences during the interaction. Having the freedom to plan out your alternative actions in advance is one more reason you want to utilize your verbal self defense skills at a time and place of your choosing.

FUNDAMENTAL LESSONS & LEARNINGS...

- Having the ability to re-create the experience and deal with a bully at a later time and place allows you to better prepare yourself and what you want to say.
- Feel free to go through the steps of the verbal self defense model at a pace which you are comfortable with.
- Maintain maximum flexibility when using verbal self defense; however, always remember that your own degree of choice will decrease in direct relationship to the escalation of conflict during the process of going up the verbal self defense model.
- If anything becomes more of a concern or more significant of a threat when using verbal self defense, then it will be necessary to turn your focus towards dealing with that issue before returning to the original problem.
- Keeping your awareness open to different tactics for overcoming the issue allows you to cycle through the model with each new alternate approach in order to deal with the person's bullying behavior.

PUTTING IT ALL TOGETHER

"Tell me, I'll forget. Show me, I may remember.
But involve me and I'll understand."
Chinese Proverb

Let us see what it looks like when everything we've covered comes together - using all the pieces we have learned about state control and different points of view, along with the verbal self defense model itself, we can imagine how the interaction between a workplace bully and a verbal defender might go.

AWARENESS: BE AWARE OF THE SITUATION

Imagine a workplace situation where a young woman is hired on as a receptionist. A short time after starting work in the office she begins to hear her supervisor referring to her as, "the stupid receptionist" when speaking with other employees. It goes so far that the supervisor begins to introduce the young lady to clients as the, "Official 'dumb blonde' in the office."

In an attempt to simply overlook these concerns the young woman dyes her hair brown and tries to simply ignore the supervisor's insulting comments. However, within a couple months it begins to escalate. The supervisor begins gossiping about the young receptionist with other staff, making false accusations and slandering her character.

Finally, to epitomize childlike bullying idiocy, the supervisor goes so far as to bring in fresh baked cookies for the office staff and goes so far as to tell the young receptionist that, "the treats are for everyone except you." Unable to accept any further degradation, insults or bullying, the young woman decides it's time to do something.

Becoming aware of office bullying is the first step and involves admitting that one or more people in her work environment are doing something mentally or emotionally abusive. Now, identifying the situation as abusive, the young woman commits to using verbal self defense against her supervisor's inappropriate comments and behaviors.

Identify the Most Significant Threat

In order to identify the most significant threat it's important to be fully inside one's own point of view. Filtering out any other perceptions or possible considerations the young woman turns her awareness towards what she feels when the supervisor is being abusive. In each situation the negative emotion the young receptionist feels is significantly hurtful, however, the desire is to figure out which one is the most upsetting.

Taking a moment to consider it, the young woman imagines each of the bullying tactics she has experienced from her supervisor:

- Being referred to as, "the stupid receptionist."
- Calling her a, "dumb blonde," to her face.
- Spreading malicious gossip about her.
- Purposefully excluding her from office functions.

Of these bullying tactics, the one which feels most hurtful and upsetting to the young receptionist is being referred to as, "the stupid receptionist." Logically, having her co-workers be told that she is stupid by office management leaves the young receptionist worried others will think of her that way as well. This is the main concern that the young woman stresses about over and over again, both at work and in her personal life - constant feelings of illness, sleep loss, headaches, etc.

Intention: Set an Intention

Noticing what her most significant concern is regarding her supervisor's bully tactics, the young receptionist must now decide on what she wants it replaced with. First, she knows that what she doesn't want is her supervisor to refer to her as, "the stupid receptionist" - in fact, she would prefer that she not be called "stupid" at all.

Thinking about all the ways her supervisor could treat her, the young woman narrows the choice of appropriate behaviors down to a very short list of two options - rather than being insulting, it seems to the receptionist that the professional way of identifying co-workers is to call them by name or by their official job title.

With that thought in mind, the young woman decides that her intention is to get the supervisor to, "only refer to her either by name or as 'the receptionist'".

Focus: Stay Focused

Having dealt with her supervisor for some time now, the young lady knew that she would need to be prepared for retaliation. She is fully expecting her supervisor to be confrontational about the whole situation. By her bringing up the expectation for being treated with respect and dignity the result is most likely going to be the supervisor will take that to be an attack against her own character.

With all this in mind, the receptionist accepted the fact that her supervisor may behave childishly, reacting with insults and accusations against the young woman. Having this awareness, there may be a need to have pre-prepared responses in order to maintain focus and stay on target.

Thinking of different ways to redirect any counter-attacks on the part of her supervisor, the young receptionist decided to put together some general replies designed to return conversational focus to the issue at hand:

- "I realize that issue is important to you, but before we can discuss that I need you to agree to only refer to me either by name or as 'the receptionist' when speaking to people."
- "You are absolutely right and it's important for us to work out the details of how to deal with that, however before we can go anywhere with that I need you to

agree to only refer to me either by name or as 'the receptionist' when speaking with people."

- "That is a valid point and I'll be happy to talk about that further, once you agree to only refer to me either by name or as 'the receptionist' when speaking with other people."
- "You have a right to feel that way and I am interested in finding a solution to your concern, and in order to do that I first need you to agree to only refer to me either by name or as 'the receptionist' when speaking with people."
- Even in a situation where the supervisor tries to set a behavioral expectation for the receptionist she knew that it was an option to respond with a conditional close such as, "Absolutely, I will be glad to do that so you can now agree to only refer to me either by name or as 'the receptionist' when speaking with people, correct?"

Having these few, simple, easy to remember responses ready ahead of time, the young receptionist knew she was as prepared as she could be to handle almost any reaction which the supervisor was expected to throw back at her.

MAINTAIN BALANCE & STATE CONTROL

The receptionist takes the time to build a solid power state and has it set to be triggered by the negative feelings caused by the supervisor. In doing this the young woman considers several positive, healthy states which she could use.

Thinking it through she finally decides to focus on building her power state from only five of the strong resources she feels most in need of to deal with her supervisor:

- Feeling Self-Confident and Self-Assured.
- Staying Polite and Professional.
- Being Creative and Quick Thinking.
- Staying Calm and Peaceful.
- Being Open, Attentive and Understanding.

Going through the process outlined in Chapter 4 the young lady builds her power state utilizing the resourceful states listed above. With this power state in place the young woman is ready to choose a time and place to make her stand.

Knowing she is ready, she then sets up a specific time to meet with her supervisor in order to, "discuss and clarify office policies." Then, just prior to the meeting, she will center herself and get into her power state right before going into the supervisor's office.

STEP 1: ACKNOWLEDGE THE BULLY

The first thing the receptionist wants to do is get the supervisor to notice her and realize that this is going to be a two-way interaction. In order to accomplish this she has already considered a few different ways to start the conversation by acknowledging the situation from her own point of view:

- "I recognize that everyone has their own personal way of addressing people, but when you refer to me as 'the stupid receptionist' I have to tell you that it really bothers me."
- "I've noticed that you have your own personal way of referring to everybody in the office, but when you call me 'the stupid receptionist' it really doesn't sit well with me."
- "I respect that, as the office supervisor, you have the freedom and responsibility to evaluate people's work performance, however, I think that openly referring to me as 'the stupid receptionist' is somewhat inappropriate."
- "I appreciate that, as the leader around here, you take responsibility and work hard at creating a close and interpersonal work environment where everyone is able to express themselves, but I think when you refer to me as 'the stupid receptionist' in front of the other staff it's quite unprofessional."
- "I agree that everyone should have the right to their own opinion, but expressing certain opinions openly can be a detriment to creating a professional work environment. So when you refer to me as 'the stupid receptionist' in front of the other staff I believe it's quite disrespectful to everyone."

Step 2: Ask for the Desired Outcome

Immediately following her opening statement, the young receptionist will avoid letting her supervisor reply and, before she can say anything, the receptionist will follow up by asking for her intention:

- "Will you please only refer to me either by name or as 'the receptionist' when speaking to people?"

By going through step 1 and 2 the young receptionist may end up getting the response from the supervisor to accept her request and agree to only refer to her by name or as 'the receptionist' when speaking to people. That may be the end of the problem or it might simply be the supervisor placating the young woman as a way to ignore the problem. Either way, the young lady can go back to work and simply wait to see if the problem occurs again. If it does happen again, that's when she will go to step 3.

Alternatively, the supervisor may argue and resist agreeing to her request. If the young woman feels it's the right time and place to continue (and she feels ready to) then it will simply be a matter of moving on to step 3 right away during the original conversation. However, if the problem escalates or the receptionist feels unable to move ahead, she can simply acknowledge the fact she has made the request and then withdraw from the interaction. After re-grouping and preparing herself, the young receptionist can come back at a later time to continue on with step 3.

FOR FURTHER CLARIFICATION...

KEEPING AN OPEN AWARENESS

At any point in the conversation it's possible that the supervisor may react badly and things can take a turn for the worse. If that happens it will require the young receptionist to constantly be aware of what she is feeling - if anything becomes more of a concern or more significant of a threat, then it will be necessary to turn her focus towards dealing with that issue before returning to her concern of being referred to as, "the stupid receptionist."

Thinking about it, if the supervisor begins yelling at the young woman during the conversation it may generate feelings of anxiousness in her that, in the young woman's mind, will not be significant enough to change focus. The receptionist feels she could accept that in order to fix the main issue at this point.

In comparison, the young receptionist does recognize that if the supervisor becomes physically threatening - getting into her personal space, taking an intimidating posture, shaking a fist in her face, etc. - these types of behaviors will be too much for the young lady to deal with. In those cases it will be necessary for the young receptionist to focus on dealing with that abusive behavior before returning to the issue of being referred to as, "the stupid receptionist."

No matter what response the supervisor has, if the future result is not what the receptionist has asked for (specifically having her supervisor refer to her by name or as "the receptionist"), it will be necessary to proceed to step 3.

Step 3: Justify the Request, and Ask Again

Whether the young receptionist does it immediately or at a later point in time, the next thing she will focus on doing is explaining her point of view before asking again. If she chooses to take time between steps it's useful to use step 1 again before doing the step which she is on. In that type of situation it will be a matter of acknowledging the interaction up to that point. Specifically, in this case, the young woman will review what happened during the first conversation using sensory specific language - giving a recap of what each person did and said, without applying any judgments - as a means of acknowledgement.

When the time comes to justify her request to the supervisor it will be important to explain things only from her own point of view - including only her own opinions, thoughts and beliefs about the situation. Thinking about this, the young lady decides that what she needs to include is the following important points:

- "Interpersonal respect is an important part of creating a professional work environment and it needs to work both ways."
- "People should treat others the way they wish to be treated."
- "Everyone in the organization is important and deserves to be referred to in an appropriate manner."

Putting all those points together the young lady determines a good way of expressing herself in order to justify her request. That will be immediately followed by her asking once again for her set intention. The final comment she came up with was:

- "I really feel that people should treat each other in the same way they wish to be treated. In this case, I think that includes the respect we show one another around the office, and to keep everything professional it's necessary for us to refer to one another in an appropriate manner, which for me includes not being referred to as 'the stupid receptionist.' Will you please only refer to me either by name or as 'the receptionist' when speaking to people?"

If, after offering up this justification for her point of view and asking once again for her intention, the supervisor is still unwilling to agree, then the receptionist will need to go to step 4. Again, she can either do this during the same conversation or she can withdraw and come back at a later time.

STEP 4: GIVE THE BULLY A REASON, AND ASK AGAIN

If the young woman believes it's necessary to progress to step 4, then it will either happen right away or at a later point in time. In the event that she comes back later it's a good idea to do step 1 again by reviewing everything that has transpired so far (what happened during the conversations at steps 1, 2 and 3) and then move into step 4.

Once she moves into step 4 it's necessary to first get a sense of what the supervisor has experienced by briefly taking on their point of view. Remembering to drop all her own values and beliefs, the young lady imagines how things have been experienced through the supervisor's senses.

Then, taking that information back to her original point of view the young receptionist can try and determine what reason she can give her supervisor in order to get agreement. Having done that, the only values the receptionist can think of to present the supervisor with are:

- Until the supervisor agrees, the receptionist plans on working to rule instead of continuing to be an integral part of the supportive team environment.
- The young lady is prepared to take her complaint to the company's general manager.

Taking these points and putting them together the young woman comes up with the following way of trying to reason with her supervisor:

- "I truly believe my concern with this issue is valid and important. In fact, it's so important to me that until this problem changes I don't feel it's fair for me to be expected to continue putting in any extra time or effort like I have in the past. So, unless you're willing to stop referring to me as 'the stupid receptionist,' then I think that's how it will have to be for the time being. As well, I think I should

> inform you that, unless we're able to come to an agreement on this issue, I expect this problem might need to be brought to the attention of the General Manager. Will you please agree to only refer to me either by my name or as 'the receptionist' when speaking to people?"

Notice that she once again ended her comment by clearly asking for her original intention. Following this conversation, if the receptionist still believes that she has not convinced her supervisor to adjust the offending behavior, this may need to go to step 5.

Step 5: Confirm an Impasse, and Ask Again

At whatever point the young receptionist chooses to move to step 5, the process is always exactly the same. She will ask the Confirmation Question followed by asking again for her original request.

In the event the receptionist goes ahead with step 5 as part of the same conversation as step 4 then she can just go right into it, otherwise she should start by reviewing what happened during the previous steps. If the young lady decides after step 4 to withdraw and come back to step 5 at a later time, it's helpful to acknowledge what has happened previously by offering a short recap of their prior conversations using sensory specific language (only what a witness would have seen and heard). Either way, she knows that step 5 is simply a matter of saying:

- "Is there anything I can say or do right now that will allow you to agree to stop referring to me as 'the stupid receptionist' and instead only refer to me either by name or as 'the receptionist' when speaking to people? Will you please agree to only refer to me either by name or as 'the receptionist' when speaking to people?"

After the young lady quotes the statement and asks her question as part of step 5, it will simply be a matter of taking the next input from the supervisor as the response - either she agrees or she does *not* agree. If the supervisor does agree, but at a later date the receptionist catches the supervisor calling her 'the stupid receptionist,' she can immediately move to step 6 at that point.

However, if during the conversation the response from the supervisor is anything other than a flat out Yes, then the young lady will assume it's a No and move to step 6. Even in the event the supervisor simply continues to argue her point of view, it's still considered to be a No.

STEP 6: CHOOSE AN ALTERNATE SOLUTION

Once it's been confirmed that there is nothing further to gain in attempting to convince the supervisor to address the problem the receptionist should simply move on to the next step. In this step the young woman can return to a place of greater freedom of choice and flexibility. Although it's important to regard any consequence she brought up in step 4 as her main course of action, it's not the only option.

In this case the young receptionist mentioned two possible consequences of working to rule and taking her complaint to the General Manager. If she wants it's an option to do them together, try one first before doing the other, or just do one of them. Beyond those repercussions the young lady has the freedom to add on other choices as well.

Whatever decision the receptionist makes the main focus should remain on achieving the original intention, or some version of it. In this case her intention was to get the supervisor to, "agree to only refer to her either by name or as 'the receptionist' when speaking to people."

Starting again at the beginning of this whole process the young woman can go through determining what intention she hopes to get from the General Manager and continue from there. At this point, her new intention when using the verbal self defense model with the General Manager may be for him to, "get the supervisor to only refer to her either by name or as 'the receptionist' when speaking to people."

Setting that as her focus and using her power state she can then go into the General Manager and do step 1 and 2 - acknowledging the situation, and all the steps she has taken to solve the problem so far, following that by immediately asking him for her newly modified intention. If that doesn't get the desired result she will be free to move on to step 3, going through each step and figuring out what she'll say to the General Manager just like she did with her supervisor.

For further clarification…

There's No Failure… Only Feedback

In the event that she goes all the way through to step 6 once again, this will give her the feedback that the office environment and group mind of her workplace will not support her in getting the desired change. From there, it will be for her to decide if this is important enough to either go outside the office environment (i.e. talking to the Vice President of Personnel or possibly some type of legal action) or simply change her intention to something which might be more agreeable to the people involved.

However, no matter what decision she makes it's very apparent that this particular workplace is a breeding ground for office bullies. That means, even if this particular issue is solved, the young receptionist will be faced with similar problems so long as she works there - the only-long term solution in this case is to seek a more healthy and supportive working environment.

PART VI

BEYOND VERBAL SELF DEFENSE

Up to this point we've covered a lot of information.

In Chapter 1 we looked at what bullying behavior is and ways you can recognize it. You also learned about maintaining proper mindfulness of the moment so as to not be distracted by issues of the past or concerns of the future.

Chapter 2 showed us how every person has their own set of mental filters that alter the way they understand the world. In fact, a person's filters are so unique that everyone in the world will have their own inner model of the how the world works - their own mental map. Knowing this fact shifts a verbal defender's focus from trying to explain their own point of view to finding ways to understand and utilize the bully's model of the world. In the end, a verbal defender wants to consider a situation of workplace bullying from three different points of view; your own perception of things; the bully's point of view; and the organization's position. Most importantly, the ultimate goal is to be able to look at each of the three main points of view keeping them totally separate and without putting judgment on any of them (including your own!).

When we moved on to Chapter 3 it was time to look more closely at your own feelings. Learning to pay attention to the sensations in your body which represent the negative emotions you experience when facing an office bully gives you the advantage. Spotting the exact moment a negative emotion starts will help to identify the precise behavior a bully is doing that is pushing your boundaries (and pushing your buttons). Once you can connect your negative feelings to specific things a bully is saying or doing you will know what the problem is really about. By understanding what needs to change you can find ways to change it.

In the process of working to change a bully's bullying behaviors Chapter 4 pointed out the importance of maintaining self control. The first step to staying in control was about keeping your balance in both mind and body. Going further you learned how to create a power state which you can use when confronting bullies. The key was to practice accessing your power state until you can easily and effortlessly re-create the same state within yourself at will. From there we looked at ways you could begin to unconsciously connect the triggering of your power state to feelings of being bullied by practicing it in your mind.

Finally, in Chapter 5 it was time to get down to business.- you learned that the three things you need to remember in order to be effective in using verbal self defense are; using your awareness to spot what bullying behavior is upsetting you; to set an intention for what you want them to do instead; and maintain focus on getting the bully to agree to your intention. With those things in mind you learned the *6 Steps of the Verbal Self Defense Model*; 1) acknowledge the bullying behavior; 2) ask for your intent; 3) justify your point of view; 4) attempt to reason with the bully's point of view; 5) confirm there is an impasse; and finally, 6) take alternate steps to find a solution.

The last step, you discovered, is important because verbal self defense isn't going to work all the time and so, when it doesn't, you want to have in mind other options if you fail to get the bully's agreement to change what they're doing.

Above all this, it's extremely important to know that in times of conflict you need to always stay flexible, and keep watch for other opportunities as well as other potential threats. This book is nothing more than a set of tactical guidelines of the things you can do to increase your chances of success when putting a stop to workplace bullying. When the time comes, and you are presented with a situation where you need to deal with someone behaving inappropriately, you now know everything that must be considered and addressed in order to solve the problem successfully. Plus, you can do all this while still ensuring your own mental and emotional safety.

Just remember that this is your life, with all your experiences, and that means you'll be working from your own mental map - the source of all your personal beliefs and values. Combining those components of who you are with the things you've learned in this book you can now choose the time, place and course of action that works best for you. Utilizing these skills of verbal self defense will ultimately allow you to both effectively identify what bullying behavior looks like to you and determine how you need to handle the situation based on your own codes of conduct - doing what you feel will most likely solve the issue without creating more problems for yourself or for anyone else.

A LITTLE MORE OR LESS...

"Perfect does not mean perfect actions in a perfect world, but appropriate actions in an imperfect one."
R. H. Blyth

There is no actual way to cover every possible scenario of workplace bullying in a single book. So instead, the goal for this book is to offer you the skills and abilities that will help you verbally handle office bullies.

Now, although it's good to have a main technique that you can generally rely on, as any tradesman will tell you, it's useful to have a few extra little tools in your toolkit for times when you simply can't utilize the larger model. Sometimes when using the 6 steps of verbal self defense, you might find you could really benefit from some simple little trick of linguistics that will tip the discussion in your favor.

For these reasons I'd like to give you a few supplementary components of verbal self defense. These simple linguistic framing tactics are designed to provide you with ways to briefly address situations of conflict where the 6 step model would be too much. As well, these advanced language frames will also give you ways to tweak your application of the verbal self defense model by maximizing your personal style for dealing with workplace bullying.

Each supplementary technique can be used as a verbal tactic by itself; in combination with one another; or in conjunction with the 6 step model.

OFFENSIVE TACTICS

When someone really upsets us there can often be a moment for many people where we'd like to storm up to the person head on and attempt to defend ourselves by attacking them directly. This particular type of reaction almost always makes the situation worse, and I strongly recommend against it.

However, there is one particular situation where this kind of offensive tactic may be required. When a bully refuses to acknowledge the existence of a problem, such as in a case of being two faced or backstabbing, then it may be necessary to bring the behavior out in the open through some kind of verbal hostility.

Labeling a destructive behavior, such as *spreading malicious rumors*, in a way that makes it an attack against the other person's deeper values or their personal identity will most likely create conflict. The idea is that only after a disagreement has been created can it then be addressed.

As a side note, it's useful to remember that using an offensive tactic does not necessarily need to be rude or unprofessional. Thus, your statements should only be made from your point of view using words like, "I feel..." or, "I believe..." or, "I think..." An example would be, "I really believe that telling everyone in the office I steal stuff when it's not true is very childish and immature. Why do you need to be like that?"

At that point, when the indirect bully begins to argue against your comment (specifically you referring to him as childish and immature), you can then go into the 6 step verbal self defense process focused on the intention to get his agreement that, "he will not spread rumors about you in the future." This is regardless of whether or not he truly has in the past - that's not the issue, so avoid getting into an argument about that (you can't change it, so don't bother). You want to remember that the goal is to get him to change his bullying behaviors in the future.

Stoic Entrenchment

A useful tool I learned from a lawyer many years ago involved the ability to hold an *immobile mental position* on the topic at hand. Being unwilling to communicate can create a state of uncertainty and really make people feel uncomfortable and unsure of what to do or say in response. The resulting effect on your attacker can be devastating.

You start by first providing your input and/or request - *take note that this is the original message that you will return to later in this tactic, so it's important to remember whatever you say to them at this point.* After you finish explaining what you want, you can then allow the bully to respond.

Once they finish speaking you must remain completely silent and unresponsive. This includes absolutely no physical body language or non-verbal communication - no facial expressions, changes in posture, etc. Now, here is the key: you *must* maintain expressionless eye contact with them, almost as if you are still listening to them speaking even though they are no longer saying anything.

This is the time when feelings of discomfort will begin for people. The trick is to simply stay silent longer than them, no matter how uncomfortable they may try and make you feel - remember that they're feeling just as uncomfortable.

Eventually they will say something in response to your lack of reply. Usually it will be either a new explanation of their point of view or they will simply repeat what they said earlier. Occasionally they might even ask you directly why you won't respond. No matter what they say, when they're done, you immediately go back to the beginning of your original request from earlier and repeat the exact same message you gave them the first time (going so far as to even use the exact same words and phrases). It's a matter of merely pretending that they didn't hear anything you had said previously. The key now is to ensure your non-verbal components (i.e. tone of voice, facial expression, body posture, gestures, etc.) are all the same as if this was the very first time you're telling them this.

Although you can only repeat this tactic a couple times during a conversation, it has a tremendous effect for shifting more of the power within the conversation to you.

TACTICAL WITHDRAWAL

Going into a situation of conflict can occasionally be risky. There is always the chance things may not go the way you expect. For this reason it's important to have a possible escape plan ready ahead of time.

In verbal self defense this concept is about having some predetermined, vague excuses or explanatory phrases you can use in almost any circumstance to give yourself an opportunity to leave the situation or put the conversation on hold until later. The reason these comments need to be prepared in advance is because, if things begin to go poorly for you, the tendency is for people to become flustered and off balance. As everyone knows, when you're in an unbalanced mental position it can be difficult to think quickly and chose the right words necessary to explain yourself clearly. Even to find the right words in order to simply tell somebody that you need to excuse yourself to go to the washroom can be difficult.

Instead, you want to have a handful of quick and simple statements you can easily use at any time in a conversation to politely excuse yourself from the situation. Things like, "I know this is important and I think we should clarify things further, however, I have an appointment I need to get to. We'll need to talk about this later." Whether you actually have an appointment or not it's simply a quick way of providing some kind of justification for a hasty exit.

Whatever you do it's important to remain artfully vague in your explanations. As much as possible, avoid giving too much detail. Instead, practice being diplomatic and ambiguous (kinda like politicians) in what you say and what you're willing to commit to when you're tactically choosing to withdraw from a situation. When you come up with a few good ones that you can feel comfortable using anywhere and anytime, practice remembering them so they will come to mind easily and effortlessly whenever you start feeling overwhelmed during attempts to verbally defend yourself.

Directional Outcome

Directing a conversation towards getting a better understanding of the reason someone is acting like a bully can be beneficial for both of you. By putting the focus on what the bully is trying to accomplish through his or her bullying behaviors will help you determine what they are looking for. In this way you can determine if their desired outcome is beneficial for everyone involved or, if not, whether they're aware of the negative impact it's having on others (specifically, you).

The other side-effect of asking questions directed towards understanding the goal behind the bully's behaviors is to have them consider why they're acting that way. Rarely do people ever consciously think about the expected results of what they do or say; rather, most people simply react without consideration and assume that the results will end up being positive. The issue with that is our unconscious mind is self-focused and is really only considering things from our own mental map of the world. So, any pre-supposed outcome of bullying behavior will be shaded by the bully's point of view - so they'll obviously see it as beneficial.

Although we know that every behavior has a higher positive intention, most bullies will not be able to tell you what that is. Usually you'll simply get an explanation of their consciously perceived goal. Occasionally that goal behind the unhealthy or inappropriate things they do or say can honestly be positive. If it is, then the only real thing to discuss will be other ways for them to more likely get that result along with the benefit of having the people around them actually want to help them achieve it.

Referencing Purpose

In the process of using directional outcome tactics you will occasionally discover that the goal which the bully is seeking will not be positive - sometimes people are just jerks because they like to be mean; however, as we already know, all behaviors have some kind of higher positive intention.

So, the question now is, "What's the purpose behind achieving those results?" An example is, if you used directional outcome tactics and determined that they are actually intent on hurting your feelings then you can ask, "What will hurting my feelings accomplish for you? How is that going to make your life better?"

Ultimately you, as the verbal defender, want to know what value the bullying behavior has for the bully. When you understand that it becomes possible to use direction outcome tactics to ask for other behaviors they know of which will get them the same thing.

Perhaps a bully is referring to you as stupid because they think it's fun or funny. Maybe they get a sense of pleasure from hiding your things on you. In these cases you'd really like to know if there are other, more appropriate ways, which they could accomplish those same intentions of fun and pleasure.

EVIDENTIAL DETERMINATION

Where the intention of referencing the purpose of bullying behavior is to help determine the higher positive intention of the bully's actions, tactics of *evidential determination* are about sorting out the sensory specific experiences that the bully needs to experience in order to know they have achieved their desired results. These sensory specific experiences are sometimes referred to in NLP as criteria.

Using this particular tactic you can often find it's difficult for other people to understand what you're asking for. In essence, you're trying to identify the bully's *evidence procedures* - the observable evidence that they use to define whether or not their bullying behavior is successful in getting the desired results (i.e. what they will see, hear and feel when they accomplish the higher purpose behind the behavior).

By asking evidence focused questions you may be able to gather the necessary information you need while also helping the bully create a conscious link to their own unconscious expectations of the final results. Questions such as, "What specifically makes it so fun to make me upset?" or "How exactly can you tell I'm upset? - Is it something you see, or hear, or something else?"

If the bully gets a sense of fun from, "seeing you get angry" or, "hearing you get all flustered," then you know what exactly they are *visually looking for,* or *what tone of voice their listening for.* Now, if what they are trying to get is acceptable in your mental map of the world, you then have a choice of giving them what they need to see or hear *without feeling bullied.*

However, if what they are expecting is not acceptable in your model of the world, this new information tells you that you may not have the influence necessary to change their bullying behavior. This means, verbal self defense with them may not work and you will be required to take an alternative course of action - you may need to go to someone who does hold sway over this bully (such as their supervisor) and use verbal self defense to convince that person to do something to solve this problem of workplace bullying.

Negotiating Harmonization

Although a few people in this world seem to be just jerks right down to the core, most bullies deep down are actually trying their best to be good people (good as defined by their mental map, anyway). With that in mind you can go into conversations with office bullies utilizing tactics of *directional outcome,* combined with *referencing purpose* and *evidential determination* to find out why they behave the way they do.

Having a civilized conversation free of any judgments can be very enlightening for everyone involved. During a discussion utilizing the tactics of directional outcome, followed by referencing purpose and finishing with evidential determination the bully will usually become aware of what they are doing and the unconscious motivation behind it. At the same time it will give you the opportunity to see the bully as merely another person who is truly doing the best they can.

The positive side effect of talking to people in this way will often be for them to begin thinking in a likewise fashion. After experiencing these tactics an office bully may learn the value of asking how others perceive their behaviors and hopefully use that information to find more healthy ways to interact with fellow co-workers.

Negotiating harmonization is the epitome of verbal self defense. In a perfect situation, in a perfect world, this is the process which would lead to better understanding between people in any conflict. Although it may not always happen as easily and effortlessly as we'd like, this process will at least provide the chance for finding a solution to an issue of workplace bullying in your office.

Conditional Closure

A common business tactic in sales is called the Conditional Close, which uses what some businesses refer to as the *Exchange Principle*; an unwritten social agreement whereby, "I scratch your back and you scratch mine." As children this principle is taught through the concepts of fairness and the need for balance. As adults this unconscious filter is one of many base components used in creating and defining our personal values.

In verbal self defense the application of a conditional closure tactic is best utilized when the attacker counters one of your own statements with a justification or a requirement from their point of view. An example is when someone says, "Yeah? Well, you never listen to me unless I yell at you!" The bully's reply allows you to create a conditional close connecting your intention for them to, "speak quieter," and their requirement for you to, "listen when they talk in a lower volume."

So, in the process of using verbal self defense, any time an attacker gives one of their own objections or concerns, you can simply make it a condition of resolving their objection if they agree to change their bullying behavior.

A good way for you to initiate a conditional closure tactic is by asking a bully what they would need in order for them to agree to what you want - notice this is the foundation of step 5 on the verbal self defense model. Whenever possible, try to structure the question in such as way as to find out what needs to happen for them to agree rather than what is stopping them from agreeing. An example of this would be asking the bully, "What would you need in order to refrain from yelling at me and simply talk to me in a normal way?" rather than asking, "Why can't you just stop yelling at me all the time?" In the first case, you want to know what needs to happen, but in the second case, you're asking why they're unable to stop the behavior.

Once you have their reply - if it's acceptable to you - you can then phrase your conditional close like a common if-then statement, such as, "So, if I [*whatever they asked for*], then you agree to [*whatever you want*]?" One trick to keep in mind is using your tone of voice to remove the implication of this being a question. You can accomplish this using a quieter tone of voice when you say the word 'if' (or completely eliminating the word altogether). At the same time put more emphasis on the 'so' in order to make it a foregone conclusion that you've both accepted the conditions for agreement.

Relevancy Challenge

One other concern you will face as a form of opposition when using verbal self defense is bullies who like to change the topic of the conversation. This is a tactic people commonly use to avoid dealing with the matter at hand. In some cases it may be a gradual shifting of the conversation to a different issue or they may simply start talking about, or ask you about, something unrelated. In either case a good tactic to use is a relevancy challenge.

The *relevancy challenge* tactic is specifically intended to help keep communication flowing in the right direction. It's a way for you can keep a person focused on the right topic by asking questions about how their comment, statement or question is relevant to the current discussion. In this case, how the issue they're looking at relates to your concern about the bullying behavior you'd like them to change.

Some examples might be, "How does that relate to the issues we're looking at now?" or, "What relationship does that have to my concern about how you're treating me?"

In the same way, you can even go further by identifying it as something you do not see as being relevant to the focus of your intention of reaching an agreement to change their bullying behavior. If they press their topic as being just as important, or more important, than your concerns you can use the conditional closure tactic to connect 'them agreeing to your intention' with 'you agreeing to discuss their issue.'

In a case where the verbal defender's goal is to have the person talk to them using a normal, civilized volume, (as opposed to yelling) they could say, "Okay… I'm open to discussing that as soon as you agree to talk to me in a normal, civilized volume."

FUNDAMENTAL LESSONS & LEARNINGS…

- These supplementary techniques of verbal self defense can be used in combination with one another, in conjunction with the 6 step model, or simply as stand-alone tools and tactics on their own.
- When a bully refuses to acknowledge the existence of a problem it may be necessary to bring the behavior out in the open using offensive tactics.
- Stoic entrenchment is about being unwilling to communicate - the result will be to shift more of the power and control within the conversation to you.
- Tactical withdrawal is having predetermined excuses or phrases which you can use to create an opportunity for you to leave the situation or put the conversation on hold until later.
- Putting the focus on what the bully is trying to accomplish through his or her bullying behaviors is *setting the direction of the conversation* towards finding their desired outcome, which can be a useful way of finding other options.
- Another useful focus for finding better options is referencing the purpose behind the bully's desired outcome.
- Evidential determination will help you figure out the actual sensory specific experiences which the bully is expecting to get for behaving that way.
- In the best case scenario, combining the tactics of directional outcome, referencing purpose and evidential determination will allow you to negotiate harmony with the bully by creating a better understanding between the two of you.
- During the process of using verbal self defense, any time an attacker gives one of their own objections or concerns then you can use a conditional closing

statement which resolves their objection if they agree to change their bullying behavior.

- If a bully attempts to change topics or shift the direction of the conversation you can use the tactic of relevancy challenge to keep things focused on your desired intention instead.

...It's All the Same

"Never turn your back on reality.
It surrounds you."
Stanislaw J. Lec

In the same way that this book is unable to address the endless number of bullying scenarios, it's just as difficult to cover all the possible variables within a single situation. Every bully you meet will be unique and therefore will require different combinations of tools and tactics in order to be dealt with successfully.

No matter what type of bullying scenario you face, there are several universal components that need to be taken into consideration when determining what guidelines you'll use and how you'll apply your verbal self defense skills:

- The number of and position of attackers is important. Is a bully working alone or are there people who support him or her in their bullying behaviors?
- The form of communication can change the dynamics of when, what and how you apply the steps of verbal self defense. Is this something that you're dealing with in person where you'll verbally speak with the bully, or is this an issue in written form, such as online bullying?
- Who is the bully and what is their relationship to you? Your connection to the bully can dramatically affect the way you present yourself and your techniques of verbal self defense due to expectations both on your part and theirs.

Dealing with Multiple Attackers

Whether you're facing a single bully or a group of multiple attackers, the steps of verbal self defense remain exactly the same. The only difference will be in how you address the people involved.

In a situation where there are several bullies being verbally abusive at the same time, you begin by lumping all their inappropriate words and actions together as if it were a single attacker doing all of it at once. At that point you then decide which bullying behavior you feel is the greatest threat to your mental and emotional safety.

When you know which behavior you're going to deal with first you can then determine which people in the group are saying or doing that behavior. From there you will focus on only dealing with those people in regard to solving that one issue. You can do this by using the verbal self defense model on all of those attackers at the same time. In this way you are applying the 6 step model with the intention of getting all of those people to agree to change that one bullying tactic - if they do not ALL agree then you continue working your way up the 6 steps.

You should politely defer any input, comments or questions from any of the other people in the group of attackers (the ones who are not doing the one bullying behavior you are currently dealing with). Do this by addressing them with very clear, specific, detailed instructions telling them that you will address them once you have gotten agreement from the people that you are currently dealing with. An example would be to say, "I can appreciate how you feel that's important too, and as soon as these people agree to [*input your intention here*] I will be happy to look at discussing that."

Using Different Forms of Communication

The biggest difference with the written word is that writing has no tonal implications and no non-verbal cues - meaning you can't apply *subtle undertones* or *implied meanings* to your message. So, to use verbal self defense in written form you need to use words that explain exactly what you're trying to say - much like you did in high-school English class (never actually thought some of that stuff would come in handy, eh?)

In this way, whenever you're applying verbal self defense in writing it's necessary for you to choose your words carefully and write your message in simple, clear and easy to understand terms. Since the objective of your communication is to solve bullying issues then you should refrain from trying to use too many words or phrases that are too complicated - whenever possible attempt to use the simplest and most direct explanation. It's best to write at a grade 5 level of understanding for your choice of words; try to only use about a grade 5 level of vocabulary.

The other thing is to avoid writing the way you speak. Often we will write personal emails and hear the words in our own head, however, when we do this we are also adding tone of voice. An easy example is something said with sarcasm; it will not have the same meaning in written form. Instead, read what you have written as if you have no prior knowledge of the situation. That might mean you need to explain things that have already been said in previous communication, but the result will minimize the chance for misunderstanding. As well, it goes a long way to covering your accountability if you ever need to justify yourself to someone in a position of authority later on.

Most importantly, in the written form of verbal self defense always try to remove any judgment statements - remember that this isn't about proving you're right; it's about stopping the bullying behaviors.

WORKING WITH DIFFERENT RELATIONSHIPS

The process and procedures used in applying verbal self defense remain the same in any type of relationship - professional, friendship, family, etc. No matter what the context is in which you're facing bullying behaviors, everything you've learned on your journey so far is still used in the exact same way.

Whatever your relationship is to a bully, the only real difference that it makes is in regard to what you are willing to accept and not accept. The types of behaviors that you would identify as inappropriate in one setting may be totally fine in another. An example is, you wouldn't allow your employer the same liberties as you do your spouse. In the same sense, there are things that your friends might say in jest that you'll find funny, however, if your subordinate said that same thing to you it would be considered completely inappropriate.

Whatever the context, the behaviors which you identify as bullying can change. Even from day to day things may be different for you. There may be things you're more capable of ignoring on good days compared to when your stress level is overwhelming and those same behaviors will put you over the edge.

In all these scenarios the key is to always pay attention to what your mind and body are telling you. The sooner you become aware that something is upsetting you, the sooner you can effectively deal with it. Just by listening to your own body's feedback you will be able to identify behaviors that violate your personal boundaries no matter who you're dealing with and no matter what kind of situation you're in.

IT'S ALL ABOUT DEVELOPING YOUR OWN STYLE

In the end, to truly develop your own style of verbal self defense it's important to consider the dynamics of your relationship with the other person. Be certain you only do/say what works for you in regards to any potential consequences on both sides.

By considering what value the relationship has for you, you'll be better able to pick your battles accordingly - is it worse to live with the abuse... or worse to risk standing up for yourself? Is it worse to try and verbally deal with the bully... or verbally deal with the system that you need help from? Is it worse to verbally confront your attacker… or to verbally fight back against all the thoughts in your own mind holding you back from asking for help?

> ***If you're ever uncertain … only do & say things that are acceptable to you regarding any potential consequences for you and for the other person(s).***

Even though you will eventually come to recognize how different relationships have different problems (because they consequently have different expectations) you'll always find the steps of verbal self defense remain the same. In this way the 6 step model is merely a frame work for how to structure the way you verbally deal with an issue of bullying in any context… such as stopping workplace bullying.

Remember that, before anything else, no matter what type of relationship you're working with - employers, co-workers, employees, clients, etc. - you must always determine what your limits and boundaries are if you are going to have any chance at successfully defending them.

FUNDAMENTAL LESSONS & LEARNINGS...

- With multiple attackers the process is to identify the greatest threat, determine which people are doing that behavior and then set your intention and focus on dealing with them. Until you get agreement from those people you should defer any other concerns from any of the other attackers.
- In written form the most important thing to remember is that there are no vocal tones or body language to accompany your message. For that reason ensure your communication is simple, succinct, precise, clear and direct.
- Whether you're dealing with a supervisor, a co-worker, a subordinate or a customer, the process of verbal self defense remains the same - it's only your definition of what bullying behavior is that will change based upon your relationship to the person.
- In the end you must learn to apply verbal self defense based upon the way you feel most comfortable communicating - saying and doing it in the way that is right for you.
- The foundation of your verbal self defense skills will always filter down to recognizing your boundaries - know your values and expectations in whatever place and time you're in, and then defend them from anyone who will cross those boundaries in a way which will leave you feeling mentally and emotionally hurt, angry, frustrated, annoyed, ashamed, depressed, etc.

VERBAL SELF DEFENSE EXAMPLES IN ACTION

The most common way of teaching techniques in Aikido is through demonstration. In order to see how to do a certain movement the instructor will show the class how to do it and then let them practice it with their fellow students.

With that in mind, one of the most common questions new Aikido students will have is, "Yeah... but what if..." - well, the answer is going to be based on the defender and how they choose to react and adjust to the responses they get from the bully as the situation unfolds. The important point to remember is that these are just examples; a few ways of demonstrating one possible way that verbal self defense can be applied. This doesn't mean that when you use your skills it will all work out in exactly the same way.

So, please know that, although the following four scenarios are experiences which I was either directly involved in or was first hand witness to; the truth is that the people involved did not have verbal self defense training and so it didn't happen this way. Instead, I have taken artistic license in describing how it *could have worked* if the people involved had read this book prior to dealing with the bullies they faced.

Appendix A: Managers and Supervisors

Jeff had worked at the local greenhouse and nursery for almost a year, and in that time he'd come to think of his boss, Mark, as both arrogant and conceited. During his time there his boss would often ask the staff for their input but, whenever Jeff had something to say, Mark would interrupt him and belittle any comments he made.

Things finally went too far when Mark, in front of the other staff members, smirked and said, "Jeff... why do you have to be so stupid all the time? You're such an idiot."

Having prepared himself over the weekend, Jeff went to work Monday morning and walked into Mark's office to confront him about his abusive comments.

Jeff	Mark... I need to talk to you.
Mark	Sure. What's up Jeff?
Jeff	Listen, I realize you might be just joking around or whatever when you make little comments putting down my ideas, but I gotta ask: can you please stop saying how stupid you think my ideas are? If you don't like them can you please just say no without any extra comments?
Mark	Listen, Jeff - I didn't realize this bothered you so much. Yeah, sure... (*in a childish voice*) I'll try not to hurt your little feelings anymore, okay? (*Mark leaves the office snickering*)

Jeff went back out to work and hoped that, even though he seemed to belittle the request, Mark would lay-off the snide comments a bit. However, a couple of days later Mark once again interrupted Jeff as he was telling a co-worker that they should move the bigger plants towards the back.

"Why do so much extra work - that's just dumb!" Mark said, "Don't listen to Jeff. Just leave the plants like they are - he just has such stupid ideas some times."

As Mark walked away Jeff took a breath and centered himself. Getting into the right state of mind he hastened after his boss.

JEFF	Hey, Mark... wait a sec. (*catching up to him*) Listen, I'm not sure if you remember Monday when I came into your office and asked you about laying off the belittling comments. Dude! Seriously - when you do that it really leaves me annoyed, man. I mean, in my mind, it totally shows the rest of the staff that it's okay to disrespect me.
MARK	Jeff - you're just being too sensitive. Nobody takes those little comments seriously. I don't think this needs to be such a big deal, dude.
JEFF	Still, I gotta ask ya man: can you please knock off the extra little comments about me or my ideas being stupid? If you don't like them then just say so - but leave the name-calling out of it, okay?
MARK	Yeah, yeah, yeah... (*in an annoyed tone*) I'll try to stop pointing out how stupid you are to the rest of the staff. Now, just get back to work - we have a ton of stuff that needs to get done today.

Perturbed that his boss went so far as to call him stupid right to his face, Jeff had to walk away and calm down before he said something he'd regret.

The next day Jeff had decided that it was better to just leave the whole *calling him stupid to his face* thing alone and stay focused on getting his boss to stop making these comments in front of the other staff first. Waiting to see if it would happen again, sure enough it did.

Within a couple days Mark had called everyone together and asked for input about what kind of seeds they should order for the coming seasons - what did people find sold best? Mark graciously took feedback from many of the other employees, including one that had only worked there for a couple weeks. When Jeff began to add his agreement to a recommendation from a fellow co-worker, Mark immediately let out a long sigh and, shaking his head with a sneer, mumbled, "Well, of course it was a good suggestion - you didn't make it."

Having had enough, Jeff held his tongue and went home that night to add a couple of extra resource states to his power state. Now, he was determined to put an end to this.

The next day, waiting until after the business closed, Jeff walked directly up to Mark and asked if he could clarify some the company policies for him.

Mark	(*in an exasperated tone*) Sure, what's up now?
Jeff	Listen, I know this probably doesn't mean much to you but, dude, I asked you a couple times now to stop with the comments and snide remarks regarding my input being stupid. Yesterday you did it again!
Mark	(*becoming defensive*) I didn't say anything yesterday!
Jeff	(*controlling his temper*) Mark - when I agreed that we should order more perennials you sneered and said: well, of course it was a good suggestion - you didn't make it. Everybody heard it, man!
Mark	Oh god! Everyone knows I didn't mean anything by it.
Jeff	Listen, you're the boss and whether they believe it or not it shows them they can treat me like shit. That's not cool, man. I mean, how can you expect me to actually want to put any real effort into my work when you keep saying stuff like that? Can you please just stop adding those little extra put downs when you make reference to me or my ideas?
Mark	No. I expect you to do your job if you want to keep working here, dumbass!

Jeff Okay, this obviously isn't working - so let me just ask you, dude... is there anything I can say or do right now that's gonna convince you to please stop insinuating or out-right saying that me or my ideas or stupid? Would you please just treat me and my input the same as if it was coming from any of the other staff?

Mark You're right... this isn't getting through to you so I'm gonna spell it out clearly - you do your job and quit being such a pansy or you can find yourself another job. You're right that I'm the boss and you had better start remembering that, stupid!

Turning and heading straight home for the weekend, Jeff felt that he had gotten a clear answer to his request for better treatment. In fact, he felt better knowing that he had decided at the beginning of the week what he'd do if this didn't solve the problem.

Jeff had already determined that if Mark didn't agree to treat him better then, starting next week, he'll be just working enough that he can't be fired. Plus, until he finds better employment elsewhere, Jeff decided that it wouldn't hurt to put a call into the Labor Commission Board and see if he can file some kind of lawsuit against his employer.

Appendix B: Customers and Clients

The bank had hired Sarah right out of high-school and she had enjoyed working there since the very beginning. All the people at the bank were great, but she did recognize that there was the occasional customer who was a bit tough to deal with.

Having been a teller for several years now, Sarah was pleased when she received a promotion to the position of supervisor. The very first thing that she had planned to address was the issue which all the tellers had talked about at one time or another - Mrs. Stevens. Although she appeared to be a sweet little old lady, this woman was incredibly demanding and rude. Plus, she came in almost every day demanding to see her account records, often calling the bank and its employees, "liars, cheaters, thieves and swindlers." Mrs. Stevens had a tendency to be quite loud and whoever had to serve her would always need time to calm down after the elderly lady had finally left.

Today, it would be Sarah who dealt with Mrs. Stevens - and Sarah had decided that she would be putting a stop to the old woman's rude and belligerent behaviors. As soon as the little old lady had entered the bank she had begun yelling about the terrible service.

Mrs. Stevens	(*talking to the one person in line ahead of her in a screechy loud voice*) Why isn't there more tellers working? Can't they see there are people waiting here? They steal all your money and then make you wait to get good service - if you could even get good service.
Sarah	(*as soon as Mrs. Stevens reaches the front of the line Sarah goes up to the counter and politely calls to the old woman*) I'll help you here Mrs. Stevens.
Mrs. Stevens	What took you so long? Why didn't you open up sooner? I could have been done by now!
Sarah	(*staying calm in her power state*) How can I help you today?

Mrs. Stevens Well what do you think? I'm in here every day - can't you even remember what I expect? I want to see how much you've ripped me off since yesterday! Show me my account statement. Get me the print out right now.

Sarah I assure you Mrs. Stevens that everything is the same as it has always been.

Mrs. Stevens You'd say anything to get my money! Just show me my statement - I want to see for myself how much you've stolen from me. You're all just a bunch of liars and cheaters and you know it.

Sarah (*taking a breath and shifting to a balanced posture*) I'm sorry Mrs. Stevens, however, although I realize that you have a right to feel that way I'm going to have to ask you to stop referring to the bank staff with derogatory insults. Can you please do that for me?

Mrs. Stevens What? How rude! How dare you speak to me that way? I demand to speak to your manager!

Sarah I am the supervisor here Mrs. Stevens and having been recently promoted it's my job to inform you that the staff at our bank are not required to put up with insults from our clients. So can you please agree to stop calling the people here liars, swindlers and cheaters?

Mrs. Stevens Oh shut up. Just get me my account information; you're supposed to do what I tell you - I'm the customer, and the customer is always right!

Sarah (*having been infuriated from being told to 'shut up' Sarah quickly decides whether she needs to address that concern or if she should just stay focused on her initial intention*)

I realize that in some companies that may be true, however, at our bank we feel that our staff deserves the same respect and dignity with which we service our clients. Now, I'd be happy to get you your account statements if you'd be so kind as to agree to refrain from any further derogatory comments about the character of this bank or its employees. Will you please do that for me?

MRS. STEVENS You're just trying to trick me, aren't you? What have you done? You didn't expect me to come in and catch you red handed, thieving from my account, did you? Now, you're scared to show me my statements because I've caught you!

SARAH No Mrs. Stevens… my sole purpose is simply to address the on-going issue of you coming into our bank and treating our staff in a way which leaves them feeling personally attacked.

MRS. STEVENS Liar! I've never hit anyone here! Now you're trying to accuse me of hitting people!

SARAH No Mrs. Stevens - you have been verbally abusive towards the staff here since you began banking with us. We have always treated you kindly, calmly accepting your hurtful comments; however, it is the intention of this company to ensure that its employees have a safe and healthy atmosphere to work in - this means that I am required to tell any customers who are verbally abusive towards the tellers here that they either need to change their behavior or you'll need to take your banking elsewhere.

MRS. STEVENS That's unacceptable! You get me my damn statements you stupid little girl and stop giving me the run around! Do you hear me? Do your job or I'll be calling the police.

SARAH Okay, Mrs. Stevens… I'm going to ask you one last time - is there anything I can say or do that will allow you to stop accusing our establishment and the people here of criminal intentions? Are you going to agree to treat our staff with the same dignity and respect that we show you, or should I begin the process of

> closing out your accounts and give you all your money so you can take it somewhere else?

As Mrs. Stevens continued to yell at Sarah, accusing her of being a rude and disrespectful young woman, she began closing the old woman's accounts. However, before Sarah could fully finish the process the old woman began to yell at the other customers, accusing them of being just as disreputable for banking there.

Being required to do something about the situation, Sarah asked one of the other tellers to complete the process of closing Mrs. Stevens accounts while she went to deal with the old woman. Although it was against company policy, Sarah came around from behind the counter to talk to the elderly woman. Stepping between her and another customer Sarah immediately went through the entire 6 step model in one breath. Not allowing the old woman to interrupt, Sarah just continued to talk as Mrs. Stevens went on ranting and raving.

Finally, Sarah (having warned the old woman) called bank security and, giving Mrs. Stevens her cashier's check and paperwork, asked them to gently escort the abusive old woman from the premises. Once the security personnel were involved Sarah knew that it was up to them if they would require calling the police or not - at that point it was officially out of her hands.

Sarah went directly into the back and wrote down everything she said at each step both times she used the verbal self defense model. Dating it and putting in her desk drawer she was confident that if any disciplinary action was taken against her she had a solid explanation for everything she did.

Appendix C: Co-Workers and Team Members

The construction company where Mike worked had recently taken a contract to build a downtown office building. They had only been working there for a few months when a new plumbing contractor was brought in to take care of running all the piping and water lines. Working alongside other contract laborers had never been a problem for Mike; that was until Nick started on site.

Nick worked for the plumbing company and, since there were so many different floors under construction, it was common to find people working alone in different parts of the building. Everyone had things to do and they were expected to do their job.

Mike soon found it was common to discover Nick lounging about talking on his cell-phone or idly filling his time standing around drinking coffee. At one point he even caught Nick adding liquor to his coffee while working on site.

Since they didn't work for the same company it wasn't a really big deal to Mike - he kept telling himself that it wasn't his job to watch over the contractors. That's when Nick started becoming more brazen. Soon Mike caught Nick stealing tools from other contractors and taking supplies from the construction site. He had watched Nick do it several times and, when someone would point it out to him, Nick would play dumb or pretend he didn't realize the mistake, as if it accidentally slipped his mind.

Eventually, Nick started encouraging Mike to do it too. He made excuses like, "The company has lots of money, they won't miss it," or, "It's not a big deal, we're not hurting anyone." Mike wasn't really comfortable with the whole situation but, as Nick became more pushy and demanding, he found himself having to make a decision about what to do.

Concluding that he needed to stand up for himself, Mike made a plan on how he was going to handle the whole situation starting the next time Nick tried to bully him into slacking off or stealing from the site.

NICK — Hey Mike! (*waving Mike to come over to him*) C'mere and help me with this.

MIKE — (*Mike looked down to see a stack of floor tiles piled up next to Nick*) What's this?

NICK — Give me a hand carrying these down to my truck would ya?

MIKE — Dude! You can't take these. We need them for the bathroom in 314.

NICK — Oh … don't give me that. They got tons of them - it's not like they'll miss these few.

MIKE — Nah. This just ain't working for me, man. I'm not cool with you taking all this stuff all the time. I realize that you think it's not a big deal but we're already behind on this project. Really man, stop taking shit that ain't yours, okay? (*without looking back or responding to Nick's reply Mike turns and walks away*)

The next week, Mike walks out of the stairwell to discover Nick going through the carpenter's tool box picking out a couple of screwdrivers. Mike knows the carpenters on site and has listened to them talk about how much they hate Nick taking their things.

MIKE — Dude! What the hell are ya doing?

NICK — What? They said I could borrow their tools any time.

MIKE — (*looking around to notice that all the carpenters had left for lunch*) Man, I've heard them bitch'n about lending stuff to you. Seriously, if ya want to rip shit off, please don't do it when I'm around - it pisses me off when people take stuff that ain't theirs. Stop taking people's stuff, a'right? (*again, to signal the end of the conversation, Mike immediately turns and walks away without continuing to discuss it any further*)

For a couple of weeks Nick seems to have stopped pilfering stuff from the site. Occasionally, he tries to talk Mike into agreeing that it's okay to steal from such a big construction company, that no one cares, and that everybody does it - but, Mike always replies with, "Whatever, man. Just leave me out of it."

A few times Nick has tried to tease and intimidate Mike about being such a wussy goody-two-shoes, but he does his best to ignore the stupid comments. If it gets bad enough Mike realizes that it's another issue he may need to handle with verbal self defense. In the meantime, Mike is just happy Nick isn't causing any more trouble.

It's almost a month later when Mike comes out of the building at the end of the day to see Nick loading a pile of recently delivered lumber into the back of his truck. Noticing that the foreman has already left he goes over to confront Nick.

MIKE Are you kidding me? You're gonna take the lumber that was just delivered this morning?

NICK (*giving him a look of disgust*) Mind your own business.

MIKE Seriously, someone is gonna ask tomorrow morning what happened to all those 2x4s!

NICK Well, if you keep your mouth shut about it then you'll have nothing to worry about.

MIKE (*considering the implications of Nick's comment he decides that this is more of an issue than the stealing… so, without stopping, he says the following as one long statement*) Dude, I realize that you might not like me but please don't threaten me. I'm not interested in coming into work every day worrying about somebody sucker punching me - so please refrain from implying you're going to hurt me. In fact, if you're gonna make comments like that I'm pretty sure the foreman would be open to finding another plumbing company to do the work around here if I tell him why all the supplies have been disappearing, so dude, don't insinuate you're going to hurt me. Am I being clear in what I'm saying here? Is there anything else I need to say or do to make certain you ain't gonna try and threaten me? Don't threaten me okay?

Nick Fine! Okay! You want it that way? I'll unload the wood… but you had better watch your back from now on, buddy.

The next day Mike goes into the foreman's office, acknowledges everything which has transpired between him and Nick, and then asks that the foreman do something about the problem. Having already thought this all through, Mike has concluded that he'll go through the verbal self defense process with his employer explaining that until something is done about Nick he'll simply avoid working whenever he's around.

Appendix D: Employees, Staff and Personnel

The marketing firm was quite large, occupying a large two-storey building on the edge of the downtown core. Claire had been working with the owner since the days when it operated out of a small, two room office above a strip mall.

Recently management had decided that her department needed more staff, and in response had hired a new general clerk named Norman. Having been recommended by friends of the owner, Norman had been brought on board without much question of his skills or abilities.

Claire soon realized that Norman preferred to spend more time joking around and interacting with co-workers than he did actually doing any work. In fact, on more than one occasion Claire had asked Norman to take care of several important tasks and he had openly snubbed her, shaking his head and rolling his eyes, saying, "Yeah. Yeah. Yeah. I'll get to it!"

Wanting to put an end to this disrespectful attitude before it turned into a problem around the office, Claire called Norman into her office.

Claire	Norman, I realize that you're new here and as head of this department I wanted to make sure we're both on the same page about office policies.
Norman	Okay.
Claire	So, I'm not sure what your thoughts are when you respond to me by rolling your eyes and reply with, "Yeah. Yeah. Yeah" in an exasperated tone, but I really need you to take your job seriously - when you have stuff to do you need to get to it, okay?
Norman	Sure. That makes sense. Sorry about that.
Claire	No worries. (*gesturing towards her office door*) I

gotta get this proposal finished so if you can take care of those phone calls I asked you to make that would be a great help.

NORMAN (*standing up*) You got it.

Having thought she was fairly clear and that everything had been resolved, Claire put the matter out of her mind. It was a few weeks later when one of her other staff members came in to speak with her.

During the conversation, she informed Claire that Norman had taken to constantly playing practical jokes on other employees. Although it was all meant in jovial good-fun, coming back from lunch to find images of nude men on her computer screen was a bit unprofessional in her opinion. Claire immediately agreed and said that she'd talk with Norman about it.

CLAIRE (*having called Norman into her office later in the day*) Please, sit down Norman.

NORMAN Sure. Is everything okay? I haven't done anything wrong, have I?

CLAIRE Actually Norman, if you recall we had talked the first week you were here about taking your job seriously. (*having already spoken to other staff members in order to confirm his practical-joking around the office*) It's my understanding that you've been playing the occasional joke on people…

NORMAN Oh no. I don't think that was me.

CLAIRE (*realizing that he's trying to be evasive, Claire decides to go on the offensive*) Well, treating people in such a selfish, immoral way as to purposefully try and offend and hurt their feelings so they go home upset and hating their job is, in my opinion, a demonstration of someone who is absolutely cruel and completely unethical. These are not the type of people we want working here so I really need you to stop playing these kinds of practical jokes on the other staff members, okay? Can you

	agree to that?
NORMAN	(*looking shocked*) I never did anything that bad!
CLAIRE	But you have been playing practical jokes on people and it needs to stop. So, please save the joking for personal time - when you're at work please take things more seriously.
NORMAN	Absolutely. I'm really sorry if I did anything that caused anyone to be so upset.
CLAIRE	Well, everybody makes mistakes. Let's put it behind us and just focus on doing our jobs.

Later that day Claire hears a scream from out in the main office. Jumping up from her desk she rushes out to see if everything is okay, only to find Norman and several other co-workers snickering. One of the receptionists is being comforted by a fellow staff member next to the water cooler.

As Claire walks over she sees the small toy rodent just barely visible in the woman's desk drawer. Turning, she notices Norman is nowhere in sight and everyone has turned back to their work. Claire soon has Norman called to her office once again.

NORMAN	You asked to see me boss?
CLAIRE	Yes. Please come in and close the door.
NORMAN	Is something wrong?
CLAIRE	Norman, please sit down. Now, I realize that we talked when you first got here about taking your job seriously. Then again, earlier today I directly asked you to stop with the practical jokes. Now, only twenty minutes ago I find out that you put a fake mouse in Lisa's desk drawer.
NORMAN	That wasn't me!
CLAIRE	More than one person was witness to it Norman.
NORMAN	Nobody saw me do that!
CLAIRE	I realize that you may not feel that you're to blame here; however, there was no one playing practical jokes on people around here until you

came on board. I've had complaints from others in the past about you and your joking around...

NORMAN — Who? (*becoming more angry*) I don't know what you're talking about!

CLAIRE — ...so now I'm faced with the concern that you just aren't willing to work with me on this. I'm not sure if you like working here but either way, I need to tell you that if this problem continues I'll be forced to put a written warning in your employee file.

NORMAN — (*suddenly stands up, leans over her desk and in a deep voice says*) What gives you the right to throw accusations around without any evidence? This is bullshit! You want to try and push me around, babe? You just go ahead and try it! We'll see who comes out on top!

CLAIRE — (*being overwhelmed by emotions of fear, Claire realizes that things are getting to out of control for her to continue this conversation*) Norman, I've said what I needed to say. Please leave my office, right now. Please leave my office, immediately. Please leave my office, Norman. Norman, please leave my office. (*Claire continues to repeat her request for Norman to leave her office, getting louder and louder each time*)

Finally, once Norman has left her office, Claire takes a few minutes to re-center herself and calm down. Feeling quite upset by the experience she realizes that the first thing she'll need to do is address Norman's threatening behavior of leaning over her and taking a posture of intimidation.

In order to do that Claire decides she's going to explain to Norman that his specific action of physically standing up and towering over her was unacceptable and require him to agree to not do that - in order to achieve that Claire has decided she will send him a direct email (and possibly send a bcc copy to the vice president of personnel) in which she will go through the entire first 5 steps of the verbal self defense model telling him that if it happens again she will file a formal complaint with the company.

If she gets agreement that he'll not do that again, Claire plans on setting up a meeting with him (leaving the door open) and returning to the exact place where they left off in their last conversation - applying step 4 of the verbal self defense model, asking Norman to take his job more seriously and act more professionally around the office.

Bibliography of Recommended Reading

Aikido and the New Warrior, edited by Richard Heckler (ISBN: 0938190512)

Aikido in Everyday Life, by Terry Dobson and Victor Miller (ISBN: 1556431511)

Beliefs: Pathways to Health & Well-Being, by Robert Dilts, Tim Hallibom and Suzi Smith (ISBN: 1555520294)

Boundaries: Where You End and I Begin, by Anne Katherine (ISBN: 0671791931)

Change Your Mind and Keep the Change, by Steve Andreas and Connirae Andreas (ISBN: 091122629X)

Codependent No More, by Melody Beattie (ISBN: 0894864025)

Counseling with Choice Theory, by William Glasser (ISBN: 0060953667)

Emotional Blackmail, by Susan Forward (ISBN: 0060928972)

Encyclopedia of Systemic Neuro-Linguistic Programming and NLP New Coding, by Robert Dilts and Judith Delozier (ISBN: 0970154003)

Games People Play, by Eric Berne (ISBN: 0345410033)

Game Theory, by Morton Davis (ISBN: 0486296725)

Hypnosis: A Comprehensive Guide, by Tad James (ISBN: 1899836454)

It's a lot like dancing ... an aikido journey, by Terry Dobson, Riki Moss and Jan Watson (ISBN: 1883319021)

Law of Attraction, by Michael Losier (ISBN: 0446199745)

Leadership for Dummies, by Marshall Loeb and Stephen Kindel (ISBN: 0764551760)

Martial Arts Teachers on Teaching, by Carol Wiley (ISBN: 1883319099)

ReFraming, by Richard Bandler and John Grinder (ISBN: 0911226257)

.eight of Mouth, by Robert Dilts (ISBN: 0916990435)

Spirit of the Sensei: A Study of Japanese Martial Arts, by Andrew Bowerbank (ISBN: 0968252818)

Ten Days to Self-Esteem, By David Burns (ISBN: 0688094554)

The 7 Habits of Highly Effective People, by Stephen Covey (ISBN: 0671708635)

The Complete Idiot's Guide to Verbal Self-Defense, by Lillian Glass (ISBN: 0028627415)

The Language of Choice Theory, by William Glasser and Carleen Glasser (ISBN: 0060953233)

The Tao of Pooh, by Benjamin Hoff (ISBN: 0140067477)

The Tao Speaks, by Tsai Chih Chung and translated by Brian Bruya (ISBN: 0385472595)

Therapeutic Metaphors, by David Gordon (ISBN: 0916990044)

Trance-formations, by John Grinder and Richard Bandler (ISBN: 0911226230)

Using Your Brain for a Change, by Richard Bandler (ISBN: 0911226273)

Verbal Judo, by George Thompson (ISBN: 0688137865)

Who Moved My Cheese?, by Spencer Johnson (ISBN: 0399144463)

Wisdom of the Zen Masters, by Tsai Chih Chung and translated by Brian Bruya (ISBN: 0385487436)

Your Perfect Right, by Robert Alberti and Michael Emmons (ISBN: 1886230285)

Zen Speaks, by Tsai Chih Chung and translated by Brian Bruya (ISBN: 0385472579)

About the Author

Born in Calgary, AB, Canada, the youngest of three sons, Daniel grew up in a family afflicted with mental illness and emotional turmoil. Having watched his mother suffer from severe depression during his childhood, Daniel developed a keen interest in behavioral psychology and has since dedicated his life to helping others identify, understand and change their negative thinking patterns.

Applying his passion to a career, Daniel received a Neuro Linguistic Programming (NLP) Practitioner and Master Practitioner Certification from NLP Trainer Judy Wright of Regina, Saskatchewan. He then went on to complete the NLP Trainer and Consultancy Certification program at NLP University in Santa Cruz in 2004 under the instruction of internationally-recognized and respected trainers and developers Robert Dilts, Suzi Smith and Judith DeLozier.

Beyond NLP, Daniel's education includes a Research Doctorate in Metaphysical Science from the University of Metaphysics, as well as training in Reality Therapy, Choice Theory, Hypnotherapy and techniques of Cognitive Behavioral Therapy.

Currently, Daniel's lives and works in beautiful Victoria, BC, Canada with his young son. Through his own NLP business he has been offering both individual and organizational development coaching and training for almost a decade, along with public workshops and seminars covering a range of topics including Verbal Self Defense.

For further information about Verbal Self Defense to Stop Workplace Bullying visit: www.VerbalDefenseTactics.com

CPSIA information can be obtained at www.ICGtesting.com
Printed in the USA
LVOW030624311011

252691LV00005B/65/P

9 781907 498022